MATERIAL CULTURE

Helen Altman

Richie Budd

Margarita Cabrera

Bill Davenport

Jonathan Durham

Jessica Halonen

Lily Hanson

Joseph Havel

Polly Lanning Sparrow

Katrina Moorhead

Chris Sauter

Brad Tucker

Material Culture
Published by The Art Galleries at TCU

Material Culture
16 February – 6 April 2008
Fort Worth Contemporary Arts

The Art Galleries at TCU
Texas Christian University
2800 South University Drive
Fort Worth, Texas 76129 USA
817.257.7638
www.theartgalleries.tcu.edu theartgalleries@tcu.edu

The publication was realized through a generous donation by Robert Sunkel.

Design: Pat Sloan
Photography: Tom Jenkins

The Art Galleries at TCU
PRINTED IN AN EDITION Of 1000, MAY 2009.

Library of Congress Cataloging-in-Publication Data

Material culture : 16 February/6 April 2008, Fort Worth Contemporary Arts.
    p. cm.
  Includes bibliographical references.
  ISBN 978-0-9801617-0-0 (pbk. : alk. paper)
  1. Sculpture, American—Texas--21st century—Exhibitions. I. Fort Worth Contemporary Arts (Gallery)
  NB230.T4M38 2008
  730.9764'531—dc22
                              2008049697

Distributed by TCU Press

Printed in Hong Kong

CONTENTS

FOREWORD AND ACKNOWLEDGEMENTS

This catalogue chronicles the inaugural exhibition at TCU's Fort Worth Contemporary Arts, the most recent addition to the Art Galleries at TCU. Our mission is to be an innovative and widely recognized intellectual and creative resource in a city of world-class art museums and significant galleries. We will present a program of exhibitions, installations, performances, and critical forums to the Fort Worth community and region that will call attention to the quality and scope of the scholarly and creative activity of the art programs at TCU. We further aim to involve TCU students and faculty on a professional level in the art community by providing an educational and research facility for exhibition, curatorial responsibilities, preparation, installation, and art criticism. The Contemporary will exhibit the highest quality work by recognized professional artists in thematic group and solo exhibitions. We will promote experimental works and exhibitions as well as more traditional formats.

Material Culture, which appeared at FWCA between February 15 and April 6, 2008, included twelve emerging and mid-career Texas artists working in three dimensions to produce both abstract and representational sculptures. The works in the exhibition were typically hand-fabricated from readymade or commonplace materials transformed into evocative new realities. The exhibition drew attention to the on-going embrace of object making in Texas.

The establishment of what we believe will be Fort Worth's premier laboratory for creative experimentation would not have been possible without the support of Chancellor Victor Boschini and Dean of Fine Arts, Scott Sullivan. Provost and Vice Chancellor for Academic Affairs Nowell Donovan was especially instrumental in securing the location for the new gallery and supporting our successful application for a Vision in Action grant from TCU. Leo Munson associate vice chancellor for academic support, and Ann Sewell, associate vice chancellor for academic planning and budgeting, were extremely helpful with the myriad of issues essential to the new gallery's success. Jesse Rangel, project manager, marshaled the work force to remodel the space and he followed every construction detail to completion on time and within budget.

I would also like to acknowledge the contributions of the members of the Gallery Committee, and especially the efforts of Cam Schoepp, associate professor of sculpture, for his dedicated effort to identify an appropriate site for the gallery and participate in planning for its renovation. For her administrative support during this process, thanks go to Paula Monthie, administrative assistant in the department of art and art history. Gavin Morrison, curator of the galleries at TCU, has brought an informed professional perspective and a tremendous work ethic to all aspects of gallery operations. We are also grateful for the support of FWCA Advisory Board, whose members include Vicki Vinson Cantwell, Marsland Moncrief, and Kenneth Turner. Architect Randy Gideon, a member of the TCU Fine Arts International Board of Visitors, advised us from the inception of the idea in 2005.

Professor Frances Colpitt, Deedie Potter Rose Chair of Art History, a specialist in contemporary art, organized *Material Culture*. Erin Starr White, a 2008 graduate of the MA in Art History Program who compiled the biographies and bibliographies in the catalogue, ably assisted her. The elegant design of this book is the work of Assistant Professor of Graphic Design, Pat Sloan, whose thoughtful approach has resulted in its stunning appearance. Essayists Jennifer Davy and Kirstie Skinner provided valuable insights into the larger philosophical issues raised by the exhibition.

Sincere thanks are extended to the artists and their representatives, including Kerry Inman and Patrick Reynolds at Inman Gallery, Paul Slocum at And/Or Gallery, Eleanor Williams at Finesilver Gallery, Rachel Gugelberger at Sara Meltzer Gallery, and the staffs of Dunn and Brown Contemporary and Moody Gallery.

This catalogue was made possible by generous funding from Robert Sunkel B.F.A. (Texas Christian University), 1954; M.F.A. (Ibid.), 1956, former Dean of Fine Arts at Northwest Missouri State University, whose support of TCU's art programs is greatly appreciated. The dream of establishing an exciting, stimulating exhibition venue for fresh work in Fort Worth is now realized and FWCA will become a mainstay in the creative life of TCU and well beyond. Everyone credited above and many more have created this new center for art. Thanks to all.

Ronald Watson,
Chair, Department of Art and Art History and
Director of The Art Galleries at TCU

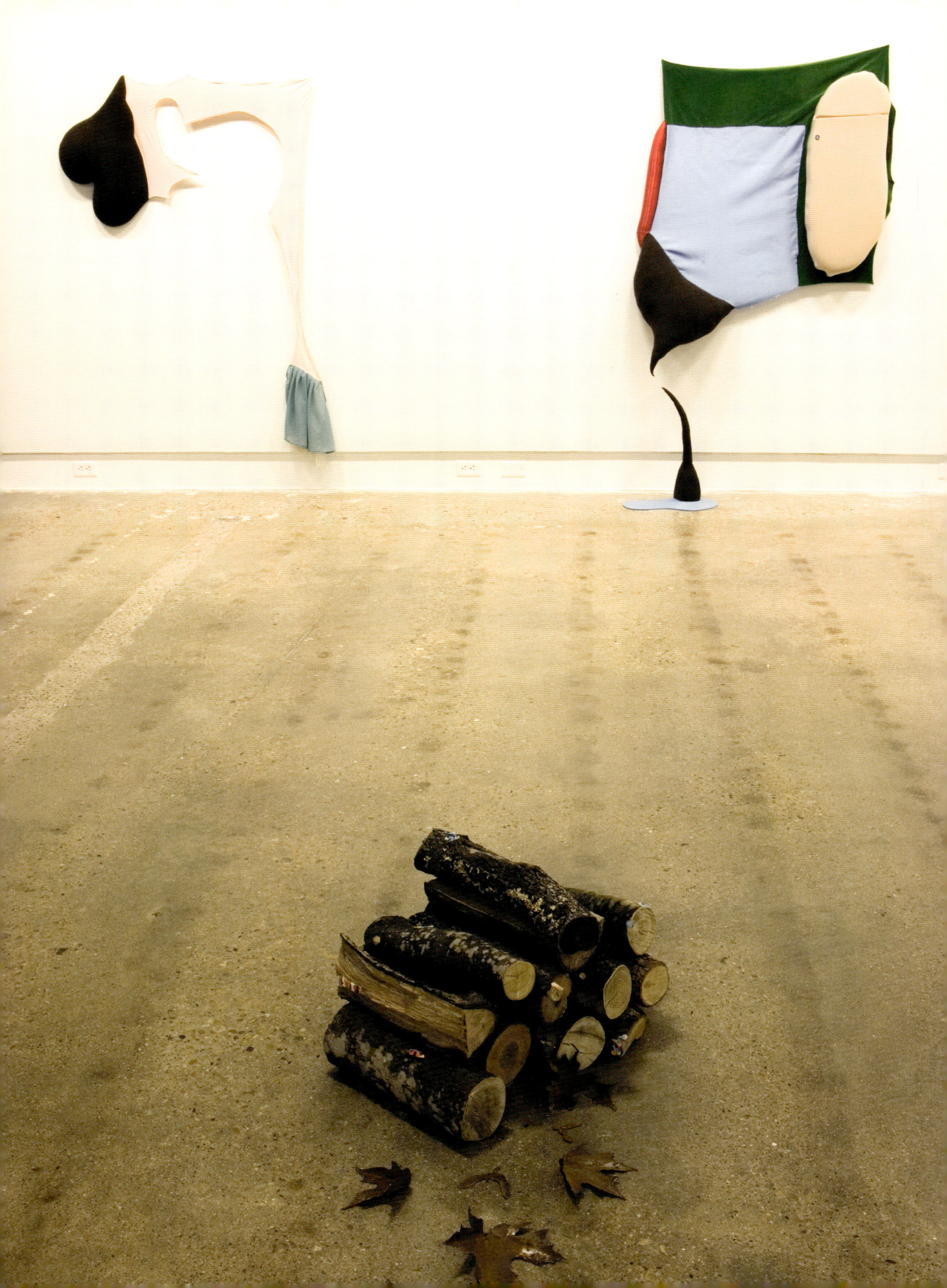

MATERIAL CULTURE by Frances Colpitt

In the face of dematerialized forms of communication, including television, the internet, film, and radio (in place of letters, magazines, newspapers, or broadsides), many contemporary artists remain committed to the materialist tradition. A common cliché, however, holds that conceptualism, which privileges content through less material genre such as video, photography, performance, and sound art over sculpture and painting, has been the dominant form of art making for the last forty years. There is no denying the fact that conceptual art has had a profound affect on contemporary developments, especially in its emphasis on meaning over formal issues and its fundamental myth of dematerialization. In 1969, Douglas Huebler issued one of conceptualism's foundational declarations: "The world is full of objects, more or less interesting; I do not wish to add any more. I prefer, simply, to state the existence of things in terms of time and/or place."[1] Misread as a refusal to participate in the art world's "insatiable hunger for merchandise," Huebler's intention was to utilize "alternative forms [and] alternative models of the ways whereby new meaning might be fabricated," not to opt out of the market.[2] Nevertheless, dematerialization and the anti-object position are typically associated with a critique of the marketplace while object-makers are seen as complicit with the capitalist structure of the art market and commodity fetishism.[3]

Recent history demonstrates that *any* work of art may be and usually is co-opted as a commodity, regardless of its maker's intention. Documentary photographs of performances by Chris Burden or hand-drawn floor plans for installations by Michael Asher are now valuable commodities. The excesses of late capitalism are nowhere better illustrated than in Matthew Barney's video productions, in which sets, costumes, and actors comprise a vulgar display of the economic resources at his command. While it is as much an object as a concept, Damien Hirst's diamond-encrusted skull, *For the Love of God* (2007), is the penultimate conflation of art and capital. Each of these projects contributes to the material culture of our time.

Just as the study of visual culture attracts art historians and critics, material culture—excavated material, typically, that is made or shaped by humans and presumed to reflect cultural values—is the focus of anthropology and archaeology. Methodologically, the disciplines have developed on parallel tracks as well. According to at least one archaeologist, the "pragmatic" approach of the 1960s and seventies and the "significative" approach, which analyzes the "sign-value of objects," of the 1980s and '90s could be combined in contemporary practice to arrive at fuller and more complete interpretations of material culture.[4] While recognizing the shortcomings of formal analysis (paralleling the pragmatic approach), twenty-first-century art critics complain about the limitations of the poststructural practice of treating art works as decipherable "texts," too.[5] A dialectic of methodologies is reflected in the artistic debates of the 1990s, including practice vs. theory and formalism vs. conceptualism. Such binary thinking is no longer helpful, as Katy Siegel pointed out in her review of the 2007 Venice Biennale. While nineties critics divided themselves into "thinkers" (Benjamin Buchloh, Hal Foster, Rosalind Krauss) and "feelers" (Peter Schjeldahl, Dave Hickey), the curator of the Biennale, Robert Storr, folded conceptual art and expressive practices into the same scheme. "I am sympathetic to this approach," Siegel wrote. "The two-party system (Stones vs. Beatles, Schnabel vs. Broodthaers) is a ridiculous, limiting way to understand art."[6]

Jessica Halonen
Foreground: *Rx Garden (Log pile)*, 2008
Encaustic on wood
15 x 26 x 16"

Untitled (defoliated), 2008
Steel and rust
7 elements,
approximately 4 x 5 x 1½" each

Lily Hanson
Left: *She Came a Long Way for Nothing*, 2005
Fabric, foam, pins
65 x 4 x 4"

Right: *Spindrift Island*, 2005
Fabric, foam, cardboard
68 x 46 x 24"

Chris Sauter
Foreground: *Bread*, 2006
Etched copper, thread, ciabatta bread
4 x 7 x 12" each

Background: Tower II, 2008
Wheat and glue
36 x 10 x 36"

Opposite:
Jonathan Durham
Greater Zion, detail, 2008
Reconstituted church pew, tin, plastic,
epoxy, tobacco
122 x 24 x 34"

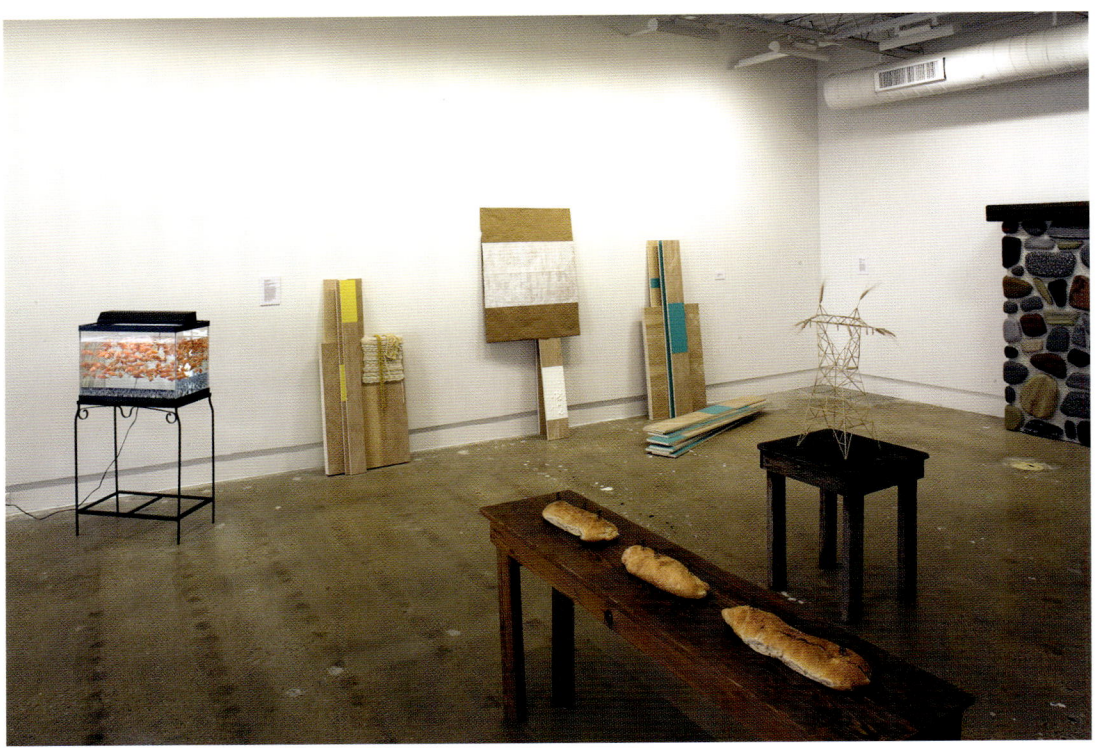

Despite the fact that critical attention has recently focused on conceptually oriented projects, ranging from identity art to "relational aesthetics,"[7] artists who like to make things have been producing objects all along. Reviewing five group shows of sculptures made from a variety of non-traditional materials in New York in 2007, Roberta Smith observed that "the shift away from language and images and toward fairly raw materials is hardly new, just more pronounced."[8] A remarkable situation only to the extent that dematerialized, action- or image-based works (the focus of *visual* culture studies) obscured the unexamined presumption that works of art are de facto objects,[9] object-based exhibitions have proliferated in the last few years. "Such reinvestment in the production of objects," according to Christopher Miles, "suggests at least a partial move away from assorted performative and environmental/architectural/installational approaches to sculpture and also a reassertion of objects, often with an emphasis on the handmade and the custom, in a primary role as art rather than as secondary elements in more conceptually based practices."[10] As co-curator of *Thing: New Sculpture from Los Angeles*, at the UCLA Hammer Museum in 2005, Miles surveyed the three-dimensional work of twenty young L.A. artists who are not only invested in materiality but in high craft: the use of the hand and fastidious attention to detail. Also at stake were surface, volume, and scale, sculptural values that implicate not only the viewer's visual faculties but tactile and corporeal sensitivity, emphasizing the role of the body in perception. A similar exhibition, focusing on contemporary assemblage, *Unmonumental: The Object in the 21ˢᵗ Century*, at the New Museum in New York, included works described as "low-tech, modest in scale, made with found objects and materials and structured in ways that are fragmented if not actually disintegrating. Its ugly-duckling looks, rough edges, disparate parts and weird juxtapositions help stave off easy art-market absorption while also reflecting our fearful, fractured, materially excessive times back at us."[11]

Inaugurating TCU's new gallery, Fort Worth Contemporary Arts, *Material Culture* includes some of the most influential object-makers in Texas. Although limited to Texas artists, the exhibition does not identify a regional sensibility, an outdated distinction in a world linked by the internet, TV, and trade journals, or art magazines. Unlike the objects of the discipline known as material culture studies, the works in *Material Culture* are not necessarily indicative of

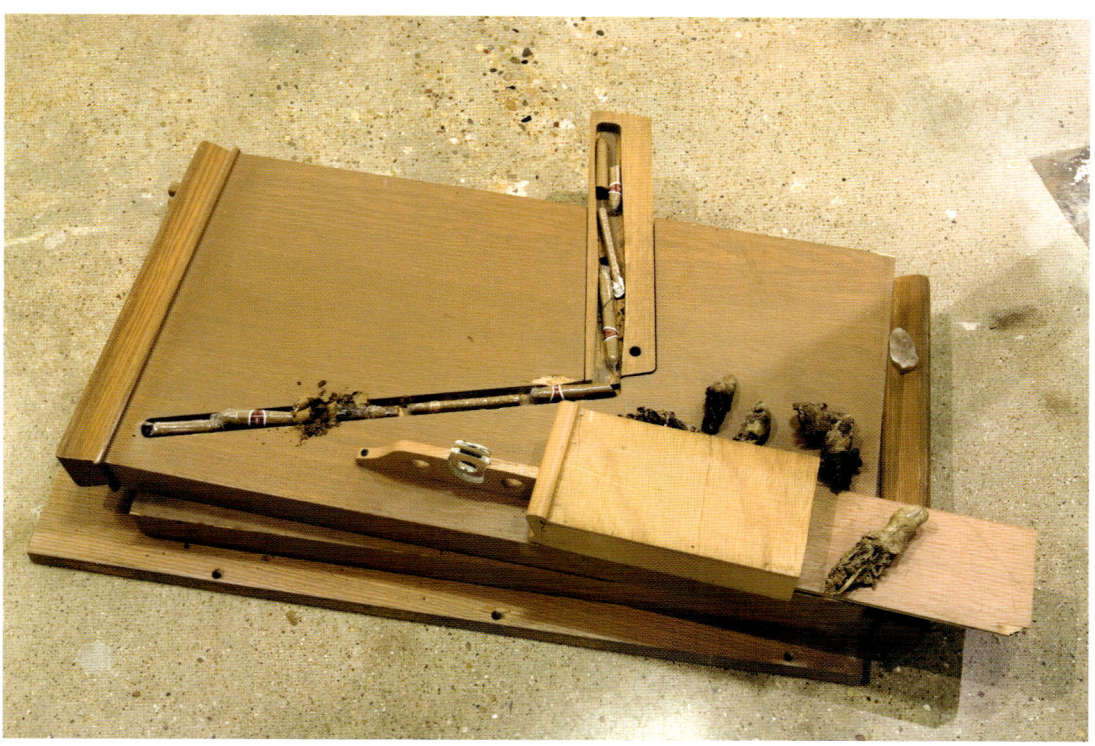

cultural behavior in Texas. The curator does not envision herself as a cultural interpreter but is attempting to draw attention to the fact that object-making is a pervasive practice in current art production. The regional delimitation is purely practical: the exhibition was intended for the north Texas audience (and the occasional out-of-state visitor) and facilitated by convenient transportation of art works. Texas is a big state and any generalizations about a shared artistic sensibility in, for example, El Paso and Dallas make no more sense than a regionalism inclusive of China and Japan.

While artists everywhere continue to work in traditional materials such as oil paint, bronze, and marble, those included in *Material Culture* use real domestic or industrial (rather than artistic) materials. Duchamp's 1913 invention of the readymade, following on the heels of Braque's and Picasso's appropriation of printed papers and oilcloth, legitimized the use of non-traditional materials in art. Articulated by Donald Judd, in defense of the widespread use of industrial materials in the sixties, the distinction between sculptural materials and new materials "not used before in art" is one of specificity. Materials such as Formica and Plexiglas are identifiably themselves, not illusionistic substitutes in the way that marble stands for flesh in Baroque sculpture. "There is an objectivity," he wrote, "to the obdurate identity of a material."[12] The artists in *Material Culture* use new and real materials in both ways, which are equally transformative: trafficking in illusion—even *trompe l'oeil*—as well as specificity.

Remaining specific and undisguised, Jonathan Durham's *God-shaped Vacuum*, for example, incorporates plastic PVC (polyvinyl chloride) tubing, a theatre seat, and a television set. His *Greater Zion* includes a wooden church pew, upended and wedged between the floor and ceiling. As if to deconstruct the narrative of the pew and the cultural system of which it is part, Durham peeled back part of the bench's padding and upholstery and removed an armrest, which was placed on the floor nearby. Cellophane wrapped cigars along with wads of raw tobacco cast in the shape of thumbs were set on top of the armrest. Left in place were church pencils in pencil holders on the back of the pew's backrest. Durham examines interrelated systems of business, power, and authority, here encompassing organized religion in the southern United States and

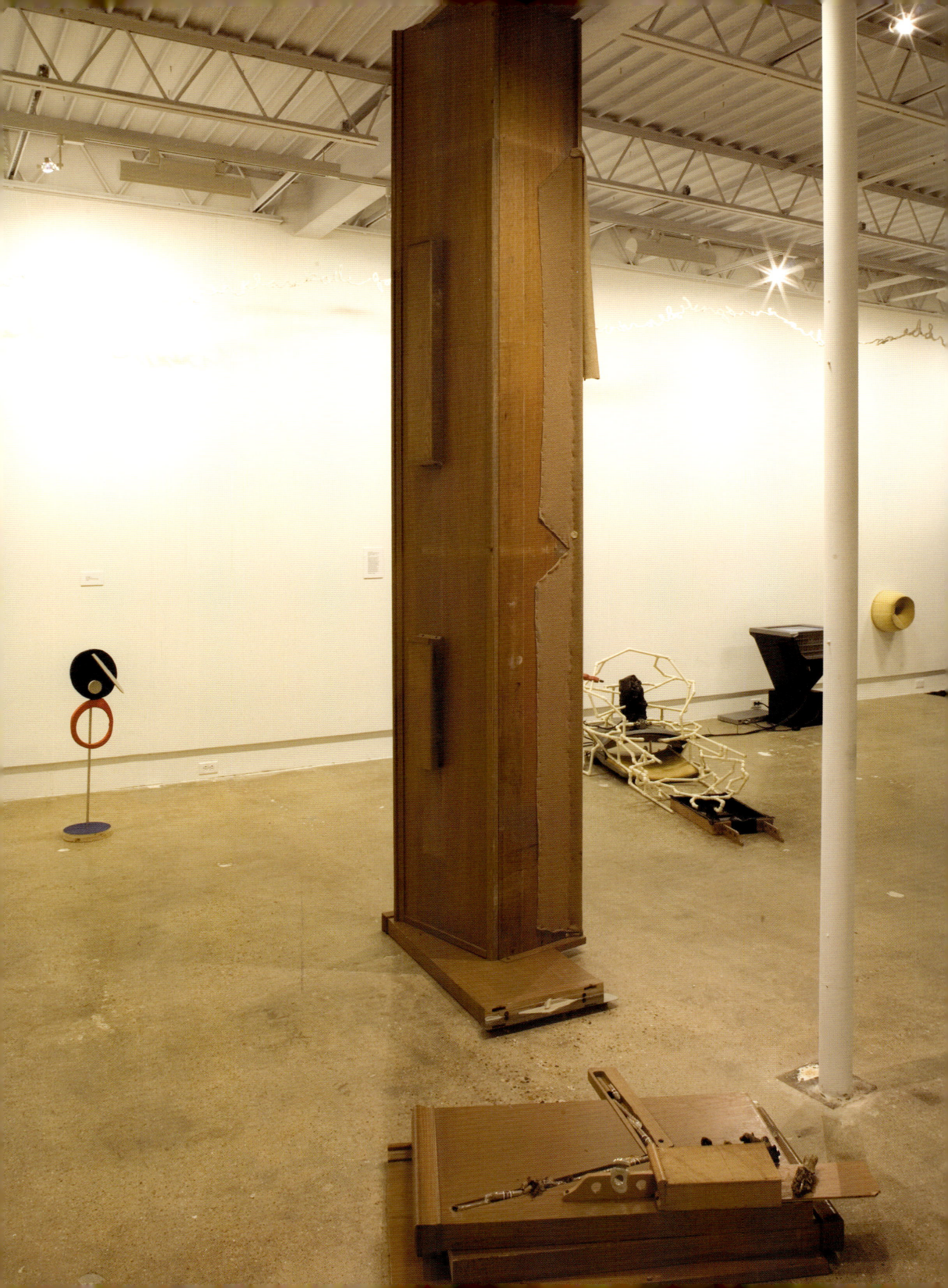

the tobacco industry. Organic materials with distinctly different references appear in Richie Budd's *Master Fifty Beef.* Encased in clear plastic globes, foodstuffs such as Cheetos and Chicken McNuggets are enmeshed in a clotted assemblage, which also sprouts antlers, chains, bottles of vitamin-enriched water, light bulbs, toiletries, and a red coat with an arm trailing on the floor like a tail. Two legs of an aluminum walker function as a support for the bloated body of the sculpture, condemning the unchecked consumption of fast food and everything else. Budd's sculptures are based on the idea of synaesthetic perception, in which a totalizing perceptual experience involves all of the human senses, rather than one or two in isolation. Flashing lights and sounds accompany this glue-drenched slice of everyday American life. Like Budd, Chris Sauter places no limits on the materials of his art, resonant with meaning and evocative, in particular, of home, hearth, family, and childhood. Uniting the art works with the real world around them, actual rickety wooden tables serve as supports for Sauter's two sculptures, reinforcing the quality of low tech or domestic facture. As a former baker for a supermarket chain in San Antonio, Sauter frequently utilizes bread and wheat as symbolic materials involving nourishment and ritual. The works included in *Material Culture* are based on the ubiquitous transmission towers that dominate many rural landscapes, especially in the heartland of America. Whether formed from fragile stalks of wheat or made out of metal and temporarily implanted in loaves of bread, the towers signify the overlay of culture onto nature, the power grid onto the wheatfield.

In other instances, the artists' materials have been so radically refashioned that their origins are completely obscured. Down to their eyeballs, Helen Altman's cast resin goldfish in *Feeder Tank/The Gathering Storm* are deceptively real. Floating in distilled water and anchored by lead weights, the fish are crowded in the aquarium, cheek by jowl, like office tower-elevator riders at quitting time. The luminous orange mass is ominously still yet, apparently, not lifeless. From papier mâché and carved Styrofoam, Bill Davenport constructs oversize props that broadcast their illusionistic pretensions. His immense *Fireplace* is ostensibly built from rough-cut stones in mortar topped by a massive wooden mantle although its fake papered and painted surfaces immediately undercut the illusion. Evolving from a recent exhibition titled *Forever Rafter* that converted Houston's Inman Gallery into a Swiss chalet with carved wooden beams made of Styrofoam, *Treasure Chest* is painted with dull brown acrylic and flecked with roughly applied strokes of black paint to resemble weathered wood. These are the trappings of a second-rate Disneyland or a high school play, where the props are signs of the objects they represent, rather than substitutes, and as such evoke analogously unreal, escapist locales such as pirate ships and hunting lodges.

Many of the artists in *Material Culture* are drawn to homely materials, which convey a sense of the domestic and downtrodden, the real as opposed to the theatrical and grandiose. Brad Tucker's modest forms, pieced together from scraps of wood, fabric, and found objects, refuse to transcend their materiality. Whimsical sculptures, they sometimes think they're paintings, either being attached to the wall, as is *Bumper*, or frontally presented, as is *Open Globe* and *Moon Gourd*, which reveal undisguised staples and frayed cloth edges behind their proper faces. Tucker's work cleverly includes elements that allow his small sculptures to stand upright without extrinsic support. Integrated within the structure of *Moon Gourd* is a small three-legged table on which are stacked a small right-angular frame with stretched green fabric and a gourd painted white with a semi-circular incision suggesting a big smiley face.

Tucker's simplistic, low-tech craftsmanship is suited to his materials, which are, like the foam rubber of *Bumper*, commonplace and often grimy, having a life previous to their current incarnation as art. Many of the real, worldly materials used by artists in *Material Culture* are soft and pliable, responding to the hand and the sense of touch. Obsessively wrapping, knotting, and sewing shreds of white rags made from bed sheets around wire, Joseph Havel forms it into

Margarita Cabrera
Left: *Bicicleta Negra (Black)*, 2006
Right: *Bicicleta Morada (Purple)*, 2006
Both: Vinyl, foam, string, wire
47 x 74 x 30"

Opposite:
Richie Budd
Master Fifty Beef, detail, 2007
Mixed media
24 x 40 x 38"

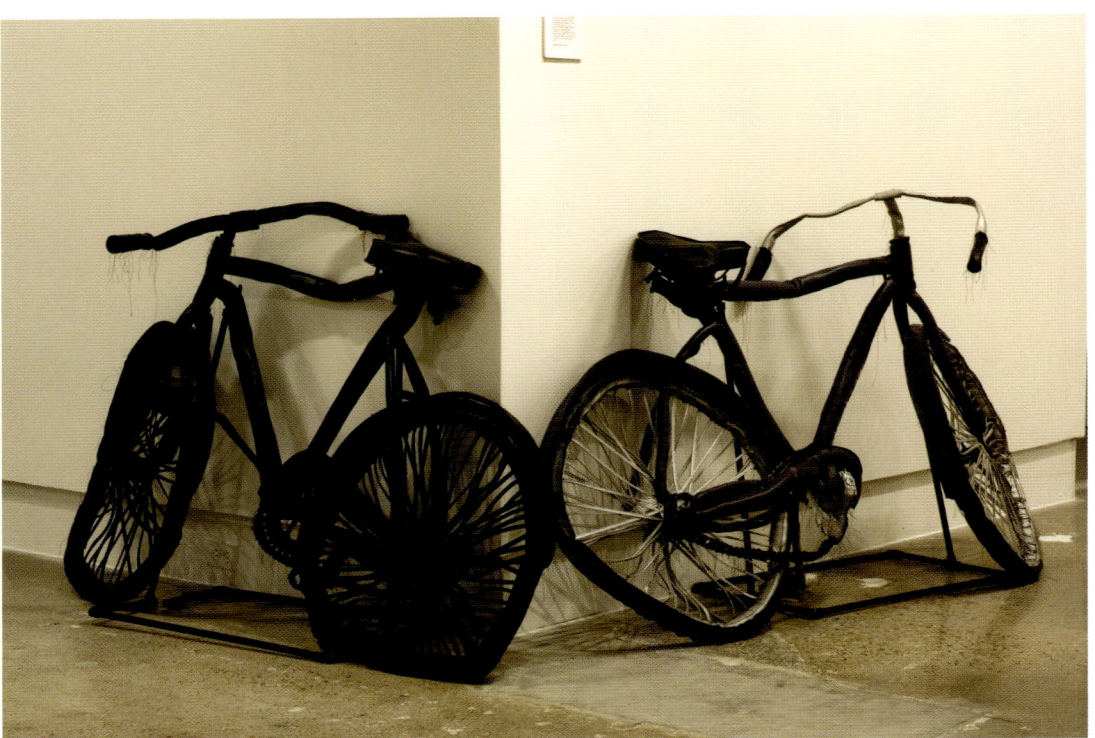

cursive letters spelling out the words of a poem or phrase. Strung throughout the space of the gallery, the words cast partially legible shadows on the walls, like fragments of an overheard conversation. The use of cast-off materials, and especially rags, was common to the Italian Arte Povera group in the late 1960s and seventies, which attempted to evoke the fragility and contingency of street life in contrast to the expense and luxuriousness of high art. Sewn from newly purchased vinyl, Margarita Cabrera's bicycles are also characterized by the yielding softness of fabric with—reminiscent of Havel's words—errant wispy threads dangling from their forms. Vinyl is a common, inexpensive material (originally a sort of artificial leather) that substitutes for painted metal in Cabrera's hands. While we know it represents the metal tubes, struts, and spokes, as well as vinyl seat and tires of a bike it doesn't fool us in the way that the resin of Altman's cast plastic fish does.

Cabrera, like Claes Oldenburg before her, produces sculptures with colored surfaces by using vinyl as an inherently colored material rather than applying color on top of a shape made from another material. Although the use of color in sculpture is now commonplace, it was much debated in earlier centuries, springing from the Renaissance artist's misunderstanding of recently excavated ancient sculpture, stripped of its originally painted surfaces. In the eighteenth century, unpainted sculpture was held up as a moral mandate by J. J. Winckelmann, a German scholar of antiquity, on whose theories the neoclassical movement was founded. Advising contemporary sculptors by extolling the marbles of ancient Greece, Winckelmann wrote: "The essence of beauty consists, not in color, but in shape, and on this enlightened point minds will at once agree. As white is the color which reflects the greatest number of rays of light, and consequently is the most easily perceived, a beautiful body will, accordingly, be the more beautiful the whiter it is."[13]

With few exceptions modernist sculptors abided by the rubric of "truth to materials," which stipulated that the natural beauty of a sculpture's materials should not be disguised by applied color. Although Picasso, David Smith, and Anthony Caro frequently painted their sculptures, the lineage of Brancusi, which included Henry Moore and Barbara Hepworth, Giacometti, and many

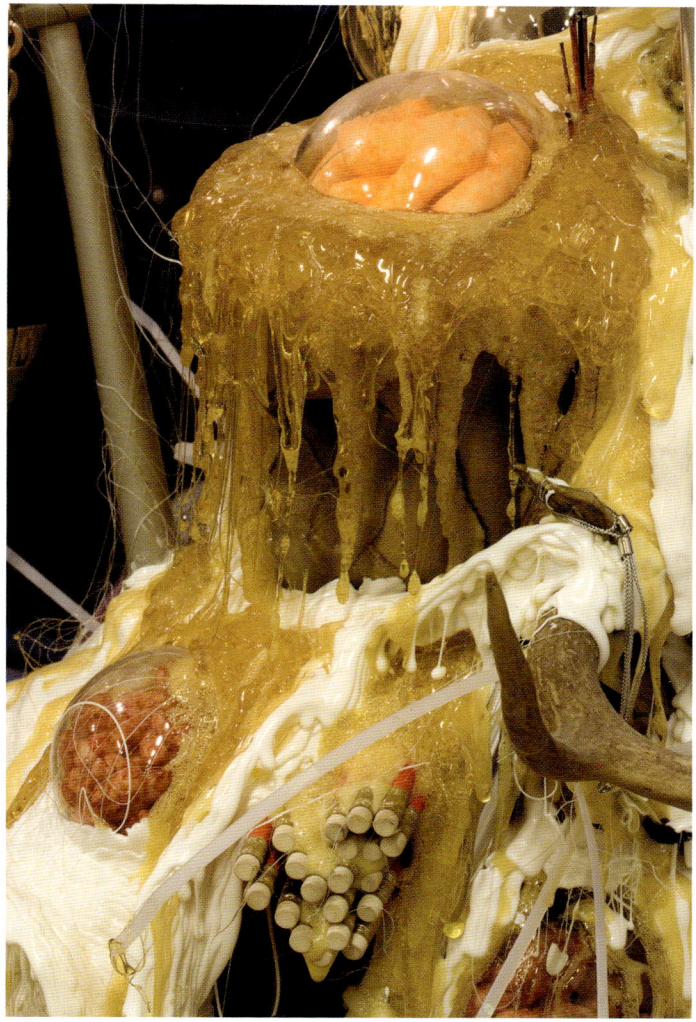

of those associated with the Russian avant-garde and the Bauhaus, showed special reverence for the natural condition of their materials, whether the materials themselves were natural, such as wood and marble, or industrial, such as the newly developed plastics. In the 1960s, as boundaries between painting and sculpture eroded, critical distinctions between inherent (the use of colored material) and applied (an additional layer of paint distinct from the body of the sculpture itself, potentially breaking up the unity and wholeness of a work) were prevalent.

Lily Hanson's work is among the most color-based in *Material Culture*. Using the fabric store as a palette, she combines not only hues but a variety of textures and opacities and a range of tautness and stretch. The brown, pink, and aqua areas of *She Came a Long Way for Nothing* vary in density and weight: the translucent aqua flounce at the sculpture's lower terminus incongruously anchors the medium-weight pink "body" and curvy, thick brown pillow head. When areas of her sculptures are stuffed and fabric is used to upholster foam rubber forms, the cloth covered shapes are made even more corporeal. Whether suggesting skin or clothing, Hanson's fabric does not pretend to be either, retaining its original identity as dyed and woven material, its associations with fashion and the body intact but unrealized. Katrina Moorhead, on the other hand, completely transforms her materials from rectangular pieces of flat paper to apparently functional boxes, cylinders, and cones. Entirely fabricated by hand from sheets of muted blue archival paper, *Draumalandid, RedGreenBluePeony* consists of two corrugated cardboard boxes and the remains of a fireworks display, complete with litter and spent fireworks. The tableau was inspired by a photograph of the aftermath of a fireworks event in Iceland, where Moorhead recently completed an artist's residency. Down to the last detail, including the frayed and pulverized bits of paper and the identical pleats of the corrugated fluting, Moorhead's sculpture is magical. A few pale colors adorn the spent cylinders of Roman candles now occupying a mostly empty carton. Labels specifying the contents of the boxes (peony-shaped aerial displays) are carefully hand painted in ghostly white, as if the pyrotechnics just concluded were only a dream. Because much of Moorhead's recent work focuses on love and romance, *Draumalandid* conjures up the remains of an explosive emotional display or an orgasmic event.

Confusing the real and the artificial, the natural and the cultural, Jessica Halonen's *Rx Garden (Log pile)* consists of a stack of real logs, each of which sports a minuscule patch of painted encaustic stripes subtly nestled within the wood's grain. The striped pattern derives from the artist's interest in charts and graphs, mostly relating to medical tests, textbook diagrams, pharmaceuticals, and other health issues. From the ordinary brown hues of the logs, typically unnoticed in common encounters with unmilled wood, to the tiny artistic intervention by an abstract motif, *Rx Garden* is only superficially a formalist gesture, in which the logs might substitute for the support and the colored patches for a painted image. Patently anti-aesthetic, in fact, *Rx Garden* participates in the discourse of the readymade and the representational uses of color. Painted wood takes on a more formalist role in Polly Lanning Sparrow's three constructions. Casually leaning against the wall, stacks of sanded birch plywood painted with brightly colored rectangles suggest disassembled paintings. For Sparrow, the pale color, somewhere between beige and light maize, and the satiny sheen of the plywood surfaces, along with the crisp, plastic opacity of the painted rectangles are central to the works' meanings. Interrupted by non-art elements—a brown paper lawn bag in *Untitled (White Configuration)* and hand-knitted wool in *Poulan (Redux)*—each structure is precisely configured to emphasize the boards' planar as well as three-dimensional nature. Painted with a sour yellow, the back of the farthermost panel of *Poulan (Redux)* reflects softly on the white wall behind it. In *Untitled (Blue Configuration)* four boards are stacked on the floor in front of another stacked group leaning against the wall; in both sets portions of the turquoise-painted sections are obscured by intervening planks of plywood, creating literal and material depth that cannot be achieved in painting. Contributing to the emphatic presence of Sparrow's work is its presentation directly on the floor of the gallery.

Sculptural presence implies a felt "there-ness," a physical sense of the art work sharing its space with the viewer. It is apprehended through the body in a manner reminiscent of scale. "The awareness of scale is a function of the comparison made between that constant, one's body size, and the object" explained sculptor Robert Morris. "Space between the subject and the object is implied in such a comparison. In this sense space does not exist for intimate objects. A larger object includes more of the space around itself than does a smaller one."[14] All of the sculptures in *Material Culture* directly relate to the viewer's body, operating in the middle ground between the monumental and the intimate. Typically life-size, they include readymade objects meant for use by the human body or re-create those kinds of forms. Tucker's *Bumper*, a 15-inch disk of thick foam rubber, is installed at "hip height" per the artist's instructions, so that it might deflect viewers' bodies should they accidentally bump into it. Knowing not to touch the art, viewers are nevertheless physically, as well as visually, aware of the sculpture's presence on the wall. Upended, the pew in Durham's *Greater Zion* also elicits a bodily response, recalling the typical viewer's experience of sitting on a similar bench on Sunday mornings. Cabrera's life-size bicycles ask to be ridden, despite their flimsy structures that would clearly make such an undertaking impossible. Davenport, on the other hand, uses over-size scale to reinforce the theatricality of his sculptures or effectively miniaturize the spectator, imaginarily returning him or her to the size of a child. Sauter's tables and Budd's walker are specifically meant for

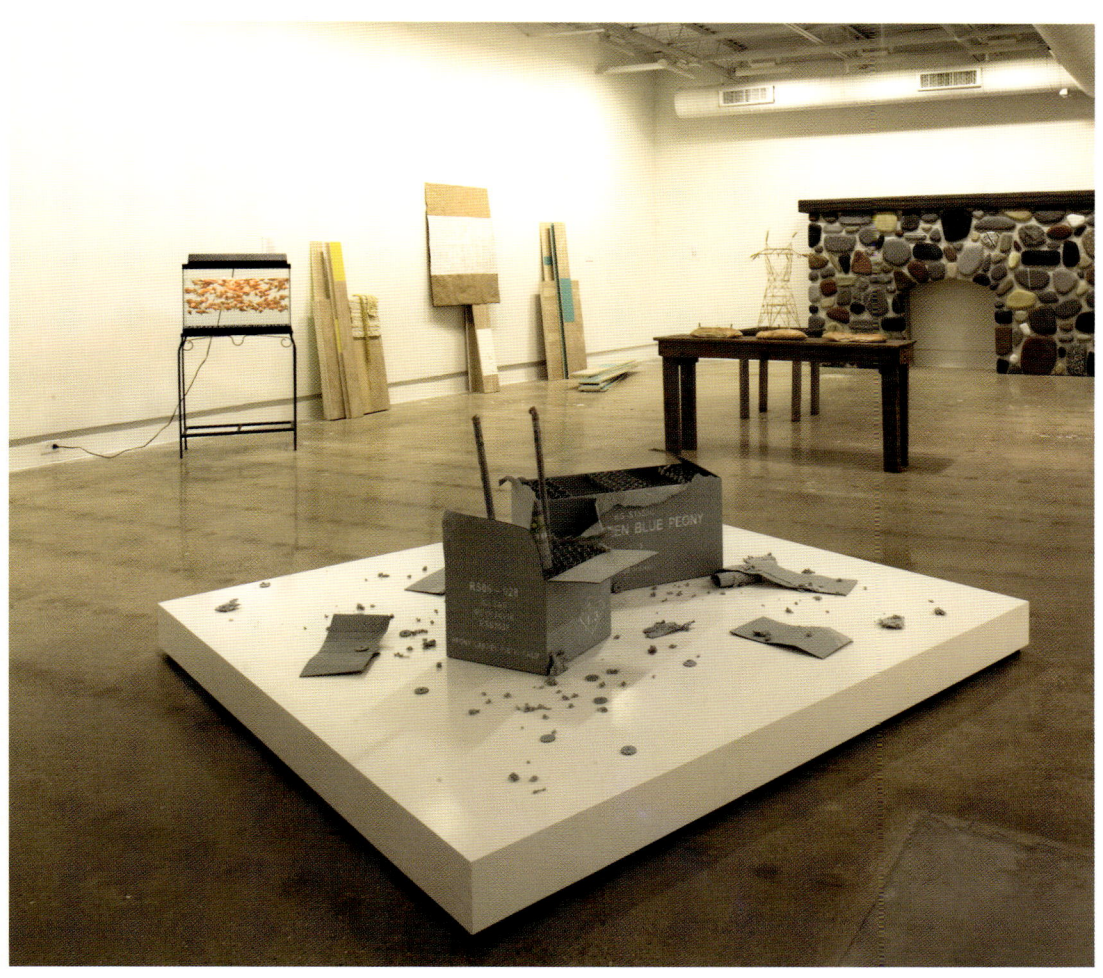

Katrina Moorhead
Foreground: *Draumalandid,*
RedGreenBluePeony, 2007
Archival blue board, archival paper,
wheat starch paste, gouache
60 x 60 x 30"

human use, lending the forms attached to them a similar human scale. They also participate in the tradition of still life, more commonly associated with painting. In still life painting, as one of its greatest analysts has pointed out, "The things we find there are things we reach for—a knife, a plate, a bit of food—instinctively and almost without looking. . . . They are forms which," Norman Bryson continues, "passing from one set of hands, carefully direct the hands of those who will later touch and lift them. Imagine that you do so: the fingers, wrist, and arm are obliged to find very different kinds of purchase on each object." As a form of haptic perception, the appeal to the hand became a significant concern for modern sculptors, inspired by Duchamp's readymades (nearly all of which were fabricated to be handled or used by humans), Brancusi, and the surrealists. (Merit Oppenheim's fur-lined teacup, saucer, and spoon known as *Objet*, 1936, is the most obvious example.)

In *Material Culture*, the appeal to the hand is echoed by the artist's use of the hand in forming these sculptural objects, as Bryson suggests, which pass from one set of hands (the artist's) to another's (the viewer's). Although the artists in the exhibition employ readymade materials or even readymade objects, such as television sets, tables, fish tanks, and loaves of bread, their hands are everywhere in evidence. Their sculptures reflect a sharp turn away from "mediated" or object sculpture of the 1980s, the last major development in three-dimensional contemporary art, by artists such as Jeff Koons and Haim Steinbach. In Koons's early works and nearly all of Steinbach's, readymade, mass-produced objects are presented, respectively, in plastic vitrines or on Formica-covered shelves, "which recall," says David Joselit, "the shiny artificial environment of the mall (or the corporate office) as well as the look of minimalist sculpture."[15] Not only in the manner of their presentation but in their privileging of the hand

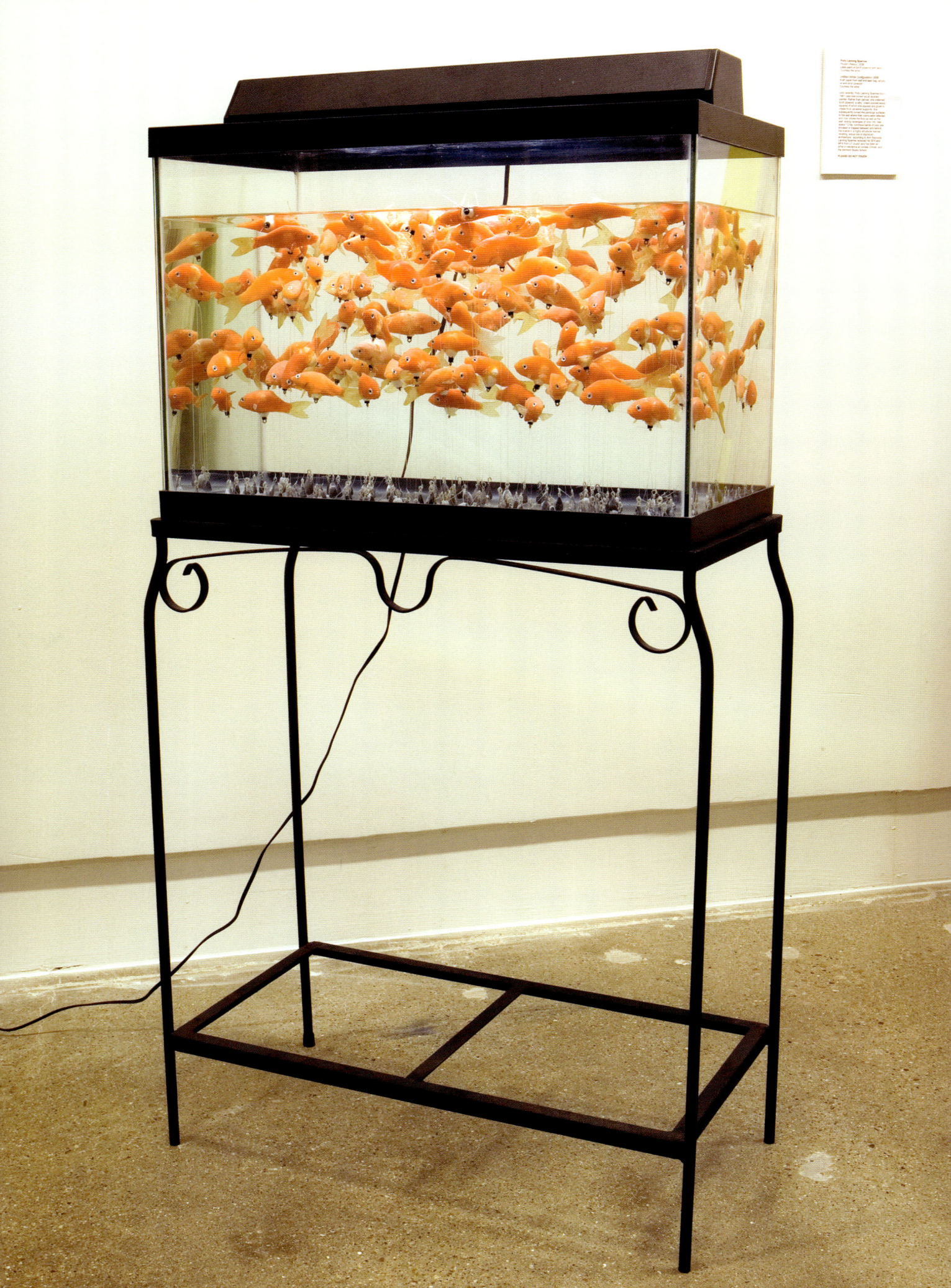

over industrial or mass production, to some extent the works in *Material Culture* resist the category of the commodity fetish. However, like Koons's sculptures with vacuum cleaners and Steinbach's with lava lamps, they participate in "the contradiction between the preindustrial craft of traditional art and the industrial production of modern commodities," which Hal Foster identifies as central to eighties sculpture.[16] Issues of the readymade, mass production, and handicraft are crucial to a thorough understanding of Altman's *Harvester 11*, which includes three identical, readymade cigar boxes, containing identical sets of eleven small eggs. Convincingly *trompe l'oeil*, the cast plaster eggs were wrapped by the artist in laser printed foil and paper, which simulates the spotted shells. The use of mechanical reproduction, through which the paper was printed, results in impossibly identical eggs. The use of the hand, which wrapped and placed the eggs in the boxes, makes a direct appeal to the hand of the viewer. Because of their small size the eggs practically ask to be picked up, in the manner of objects in a still life. Halonen's *Untitled (defoliated)*, a set of seven rusted steel leaves installed in and around her *Rx Garden*, make a similar appeal. Although they are shown on the floor without the interference of a base or container, their size and powdery brown surfaces elicit a haptic— rather than optical—understanding.

In other works in the exhibition, the handicraft employed in creating the works is a crucial aspect of the works' representation of or reference to the subject matter of labor. As a resident of El Paso, Margarita Cabrera focuses on border issues, including immigration and, especially, exploitation by the maquiladora, where cheap Mexican labor, overseen by American industries, produces goods to be exported to the United States. She has transformed dark green border patrol uniforms into cactus plants. Issued from her needle are kitchen appliances such as blenders, backpacks, and even life-size Hummer automobiles, all made from pliant, colored vinyl. Her black and purple bicycles, *Bicicleta Negra* and *Bicicleta Morada*, were inspired by the ubiquitous mode of transportation used by border residents. Ostensibly mere representations of common objects, Cabrera's bicycles participate in a dialogue that is currently one of the country's most contentious: undocumented immigration and the outsourcing of jobs. Sewn with her own hands using a sewing machine, the rickety sculptures droop on their stands, clearly unable to support, much less propel, a rider through dusty streets or down the highway to the factory. An alternate form of representing labor, though one no less political, is seen in Havel's *Drinks are boiling. Iced drinks are boiling*, which is a literally unraveling ball of words spun across the gallery as if from the hand of the poet, John Berryman, himself. The words are formed of wire, hand-wrapped with small fabric strips, a process that is obviously labor-intensive. Evoking the repetitive nature of housework, including laundry and sewing, Havel employs domestic materials, such as sheets, curtains, and men's dress shirts. Like Eva Hesse, he utilizes processes of wrapping, binding, and tying as metaphors for caretaking and nurturing, roles stereotypically attributed to women.

In Katrina Moorhead's work, issues of labor are layered and multifaceted. The cartons of exploded fireworks, decorated with dragons, recall the original's source in Chinese manufacturing, most likely utilizing an assembly line staffed with numerous workers, while the labor-intensive, and singularly individual, task of exactly reproducing the cardboard objects by hand is daunting to consider. Sauter's devotion to handicraft and intimate detail—stringing the miniature towers with threads and gluing together the thin shafts of wheat in the construction of *Tower II*—is radically distinct from Budd's fondness for slapdash tinkering. Budd functions like a mad scientist, assembling a robotic critique of gluttonous consumption. Tucker is a casual *bricoleur*, precariously stacking unrelated objects that are on the verge of collapse or exhibiting so little workmanship that, for example, the foam rubber cushion of *Bumper* seems to have got up and attached itself to the wall without assistance.

This exhibition includes a group of the Texas artists who are working in three-dimensions using real or found materials that engage the hand. As it turned out, representation and narrative are also of considerable importance. Even the primarily formal works of Polly Lanning Sparrow, which are concerned with architecture, construction, and domesticity, and Lily Hanson, which conjure the body, clothing and, in the case of *Phil's Form*, an upholstered rocking horse (that is, a piece of furniture scaled for a child), cannot be categorized as purely abstract. The subjects investigated range from the personal to the political. Reflecting a commitment to the former, Altman's works are nearly always inspired by personal circumstances, and especially by her devotion to the welfare of animals. The eggs in *Harvester 11* represent the eggs laid by chickens in her Fort Worth backyard, which she was able to attribute—based on their size, color, and speckling—to individual birds.[17] Also highly personal in origin, Havel's *Drinks are boiling. Iced drinks are boiling* conveys his fondness for the poetry of John Berryman (1914 – 1972), a revered mid-century American author. As Havel recalls, "I chose this phrase from the book *The Dream Songs* because I had spent many years remembering it incorrectly. I placed the punctuation in the wrong place. The word 'Iced' I had connected to the first sentence but it actually begins the second sentence. So for me once I realized this it became a kind of hinge where it belonged to either sentence, could shift between the two sentences, or be considered independently from either sentence as its own element." The torn bed sheets used in his work evoke the state of dreaming, in between sleep and wakefulness.[18] Due to the distorted and tangled wire and partially legible shadows cast by the words, the clear and complete text of the poem is as elusive as an interrupted dream.

No less complex in its subject is Durham's *God-shaped Vacuum*, which includes a recycling water fountain constructed out of PVC. Fading in and out on the screen of a television set are still images of a surveillance camera filming its reflection in a mirror and an infamous photograph of torture in which an American soldier sits on the back of an Iraqi prisoner at Abu Ghraib. Nearby, water courses through the sled-like fountain contraption, placed a few feet from the TV. As Durham explained, "The PVC alludes to the figures [in the photograph] but also creates this closed off, impenetrable system. I was interested in creating a structure (perhaps the dominant political structure) that is trying to contain or suppress itself and the narratives that lie beneath." The PVC represents the inescapable circuitry that characterizes political systems and structures, such as the prisons and the military, "so encoded in [their] own rules that someone would not be able to make an individual moral decision about right and wrong."[19]

Based on the fact that story-telling is nearly ubiquitous in *Material Culture*, the sculptures in the exhibition required a degree of "mental space" around them to prevent a kind of collision of expansive narratives. Unlike a one-person exhibition or a thematic survey, the sculptures' physical presences in *Material Culture* were complicated by the viewer's attempts to unravel a variety of interpretations and concepts. Densely installed, the exhibition was characterized by a cacophony of voices, each affecting the next, and occluding a simplistic and unified point of view. Perhaps in the end, it reflects the generally fragmentary and competitive state of contemporary culture, propelled by consumption, carried aloft on illusion, and deeply materialistic.

1   Artist's statement, *January 5 – 31, 1969* (New York: Seth Siegelaub, 1969), n. p.

2   Douglas Huebler, "Sabotage or Trophy: Advance or Retreat?" *Artforum* 20 (May 1982): 76.

3   See Hal Foster, "The Future of an Illusion, Or the Contemporary Artist as Cargo Cultist," in *Endgame: Reference and Simulation in Recent Painting and Sculpture*, by Yve-Alain Bois et al. (Cambridge: MIT Press, 1986), 91 – 105. According to Foster, "The work of art in capitalist society cannot escape the status of a commodity." See also Benjamin H. D. Buchloh, "Michael Asher and the Condition of Modernist Sculpture," in *Neo-Avant Garde and Culture Industry: Essays on European and American Art from 1955 to 1975* (Cambridge: MIT Press, 2001), 1 – 12.

4   Jean-Pierre Warnier, "Material Culture Meaning or Handling?" *Current Anthropology* 48 (October 2007): 770.

5   See Yve-Alain Bois, Denis Hollier, Rosalind Krauss, and Hubert Damisch, "A Conversation with Hubert Damisch," *October*, no. 85 (Summer 1998): 12.

6   Katy Siegel, "The Buck Stops Here," *Artforum* 46 (September 2007): 391 – 92.

7   See Nicholas Bourriaud, *Relational Aesthetics* (Dijon: Les presses du réel, 2002), a trendy analysis of contemporary project-based art, including works by Rikrit Tiravanija, Gabriel Orozco, et al.

8   Roberta Smith, "In These Shows, the Material is the Message," *New York Times*, 10 August 2007, http://www.nytimes.com/2007/08/10/arts/design/10mate.html.

9   The problem with the rubric of visual culture, in contrast to art history, according to Thomas Crow, is that "it accepts without question the view that art is to be defined by its working exclusively through the optical faculties." Thomas Crow, et al., "Visual Culture Questionnaire," *October,* no. 77 (Summer 1996): 35. As a discipline, visual culture reflects the contemporary interest in images over objects and the use of the eye over the body in the act of perception.

10 Christopher Miles, "A Thing for Things," in *Thing: New Sculpture from Los Angeles*, by James Elaine, Aimee Chang, and Christopher Miles (Los Angeles: Armand Hammer Museum of Art, 2005), 10.

11 Roberta Smith, "Unmonumental: The Object in the 21st Century," *New York Times,* 30 November 2007, http://www.nytimes.com/2007/11/30/arts/design/30newm.html.

12 Donald Judd, "Specific Objects," in *Complete Writings: 1959 – 1975* (Halifax: Nova Scotia College of Art and Design, 1975), 80.

13 Winckelmann's point of view is characteristic of the many racist (sexist, classicist, etc.) presumptions of Enlightenment humanism. Johann Joachim Winckelmann, *History of Ancient Art*, trans. G. Henry Lodge (New York: Frederick Ungar, 1968), 198. See my *Chromaform: Color in Sculpture* (San Antonio: University of Texas at San Antonio, 1998) for a discussion of the history of polychromy.

14 Robert Morris, "Notes on Sculpture, Part II," in *Minimal Art: A Critical Anthology*, ed. Gregory Battcock (New York: Praeger, 1968), 231.

15 David Joselit, "Modern Leisure," in *Endgame: Reference and Simulation in Recent Painting and Sculpture*, 80.

16 Foster, "The Future of an Illusion," 92.

17 Conversation with Helen Altman, 27 March 2008.

18 Email from Joseph Havel, 15 April 2008.

19 Interview with Priyah Bhatnagar, *Core Artists in Residence 2007* (Houston: Museum of Fine Arts, 2007), n. p.

AUTHOR'S BIOGRAPHY

Frances Colpitt is the Deedie Potter Rose Chair of Art History at Texas Christian University. She holds a B.F.A. (Painting) and a M.A. (Humanities) from the University of Tulsa, and a Ph.D. (Art History) from the University of Southern California. Dr. Colpitt has published extensively and her books include *Minimal Art: The Critical Perspective*, *Abstract Options,* and *Abstract Art in the Late Twentieth Century*. She is a corresponding editor for *Art in America* and a regular contributor to *artUS*. Dr. Colpitt has been the curator of numerous exhibitions, which have appeared in such venues as the Phoenix Art Museum, the University Art Museum (UCSB), Fisher Gallery (USC), Blue Star Art Space, Artpace, and the UTSA Art Gallery.

Haunted Material by Kirstie Skinner

"Material" is a category denoting physical substance, and in as much as anything can be said to exist, material things do. "Material culture" describes the interrelations between people and material things and is the basis of academic disciplines such as social anthropology and museum studies, which testify to the fact that material things cannot be understood independently of an immaterial dimension—their use and significance within a given society is determined by their associations as much as their material substance. Private associations accrue from an individual's previous experience, and public associations from a wider consensus. If the "immaterial" is a category at all then, its contents are difficult to define—ideas are fluid and transient rather than relatively fixed and predictable as substances are. Immaterial "objects" are impossible to limit and quantify with any degree of certainty, and their existence is entirely speculative; ideas are as souls, specters, avatars. Delineating the realm of the immaterial is largely the preoccupation of philosophy and religion.

According to the Platonic tradition, *idea* supersedes base materiality in approaching the real (as opposed to the ostensible) "truth." Now, with the death of God and the rise of the rule of science, ostensible truth—material fact—is the only "truth" left. The lament that our culture is "increasingly dematerialized" seems to arise from a fear that we might ultimately become untethered from these material "truths" and thus deprived of any measure of authenticity. Within the cycles of consumption that define capitalism, for instance, the fluid "symbolic value" of a thing (an immaterial supplement) has come to overshadow its more stable "use value" (the value ascribed to its material substance and function). As human relations are increasingly conducted remotely, in virtual space, their rootedness in fixed forms and identities is withering. In this context the immaterial is no longer conceived as a form of sublime transcendence, but as an increasingly ubiquitous form of psychotic disconnectedness.

These anxieties have underpinned a great deal of artistic practice since the 1960s, when a commitment to concrete materiality vied with manifestoes of dematerialization as appropriate modes for advanced art. Despite taking up different positions within this polemic, pop artists, minimalists, and conceptual artists were all preoccupied by the same question: How should art deal with the increasing dematerialization of things in an economy driven by perpetual attraction and distraction? Faced with this predicament, artists were forced to choose: either to ward off the threat by recuperating and celebrating the material elements of material culture, or else to embrace the freedom from corporeal limitations that the immaterial offers, and disregard notions of truth and authenticity altogether. Although it has been widely conceded since the 1960s that "authenticity" in art and literature is a mythical concept, many people still rely on an authentic correspondence between material things and an independent "reality." Subsequent generations have become more inured to the dematerialized aspects of quotidian experience, but dealing with the implications of dematerialization remains a key challenge.

The curator of *Material Culture*, Frances Colpitt, has explained that the exhibition consists of a celebration of material culture in the face of dematerialization. The works gathered together have a direct material presence, in contrast to more allusive depictions contained in graphic and photographic work, and the more cerebral and emotional processes evoked by performance and conceptual projects. Are we to think of these works, then, as material counterpoints to immaterial illusions and ideas? If so, the distinction should be understood not as absolute, but as one of degree—representations still feature, albeit in three dimensions, and inevitably, conceptual processes are evident. In order to become art, source objects drawn from contemporary material culture must undergo a process of displacement, either figuratively (an object is scrutinized and re-created, and the materiality of the original is displaced) or literally (an object is plundered and re-displayed, displaced from its original context). Thus, hard objects have been re-imagined

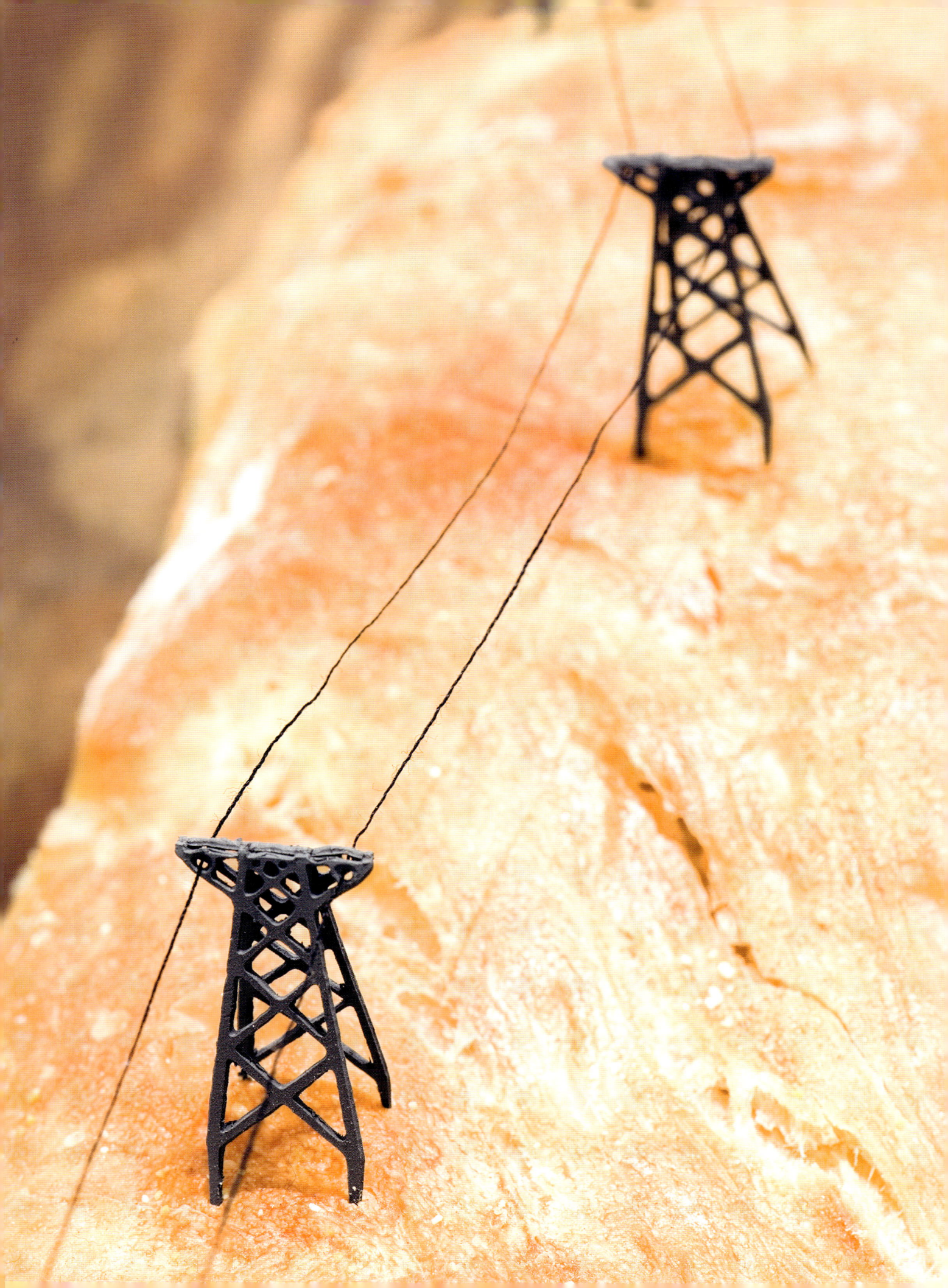

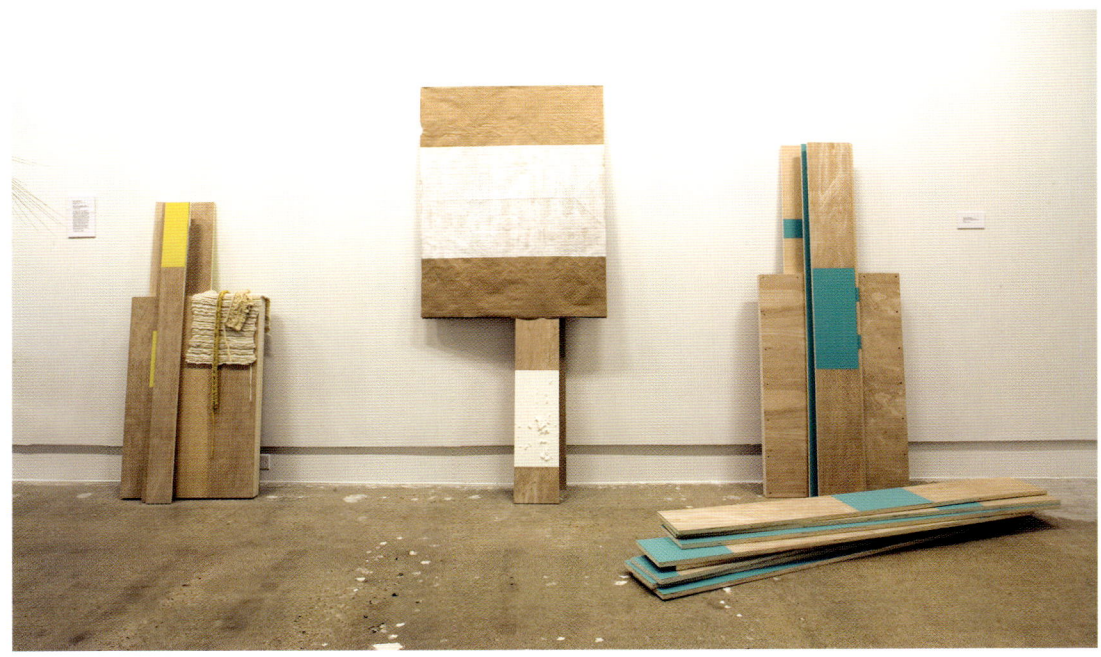

as soft and vice versa, craft techniques have been deployed in re-constructing a whole array of familiar objects, and miniature and gigantic transformations have been effected. Found objects have been collected, arranged, employed in assemblages, and turned into abstractions; they have been resituated and recombined—sometimes in ordered topologies, sometimes in monstrous agglomerations.

For such practices that celebrate material culture, we might distinguish, as Donald Judd did, between those preoccupied with *material* and those primarily interested in *culture*. Considering his own abstract minimalist geometries, it may seem surprising that Donald Judd should have championed the work of Claes Oldenburg, who, he said, created giant "grossly anthropomorphized" versions of manmade things out of flaccid plastic.[1] In his writings, Judd drew a contrast between "George Brecht and Robert Morris" who "use[d] real objects and depend[ed] on the viewer's knowledge of these objects,"[2] and Oldenburg, who "exaggerate[d] the accepted or chosen form and turn[ed] it into one of his own."[3] Oldenberg succeeded in moving so far beyond the object he was "representing" that any purported mimetic relationship was deliberately and effectively undermined. As far as Judd was concerned, cultural references distracted the viewer from the here and now, and he "wanted to get rid of all those extraneous meanings—connections to things that didn't mean anything to the art."[4] He felt that extraordinary, unexpected forms and strongly specific materials served to re-invest the artistic encounter with surprise and singularity. Viewers were forced to begin by questioning how such forms should be navigated and explored—focusing all their attention and awareness on *what* was present *in* the present. Praising a work by Lee Bontecou, for instance, Judd wrote, "Rather than inducing idealization and generalization and being allusive, it excludes. The work asserts its own existence, form and power. It becomes an object in its own right."[5] Expulsion of allusion was, for Judd, the means of resisting the dematerialized promiscuity of thought in the distracted culture of the 1960s. He attested that "[t]hings that exist, exist, and everything is on their side. They're here, which is pretty puzzling. Nothing can be said of things that don't exist…. Everything is equal, just existing, and the values and interests they have are only adventitious."[6] Studiously avoiding forms and colors that might bring cultural associations with them, Judd hoped that his own works *were*, and were *only*, their distinct and concrete quality.

What is fascinating, though, is what happens when the materiality of a thing is brought to prominence in this way. Think, for example, of the nausea that overcomes Jean-Paul Sartre's Antoine Roquentin as he thinks he sees material things (crumpled paper, a rock, a root) divested of the language and conceptual structure that have hitherto contained them.[7] Try to expel "extraneous" meanings and "adventitious" qualities—those things that for Judd "don't exist"—and enigmas necessarily arise in their place. Disconnected from obvious, habitual, or sanctioned associations, an object inevitably becomes receptive to new associations. This openness is disturbing on two counts. It demonstrates that the object is in fact susceptible to endless possibility, and it is precisely the possibility of being or meaning anything at all that threatens a thing's integrity in a dematerialized world; and it insinuates that the object may be subject to an unknown conceptual structure, alien to the viewer's own. Material things that resist incorporation into a familiar world of meaning thus acquire an *unheimlich* aura.

It is clear from contemporaneous reviews that many people found the mysterious, obstinate silence of Judd's blank sculptural forms to be unsettling. Several commentators attested to becoming self-conscious in the presence of what they construed to be the hidden or secret "life" of the object. This self-consciousness was presented either positively, as a force for greater criticality and self-awareness on the part of the viewer, or negatively, as an alienating experience. Michael Fried later remembered his dislike of such sculpture: "My critique of the literalist address to the viewer's body was […] that literalism theatricalised the body, put it endlessly on stage, made it uncanny or opaque to itself, hollowed it out, deadened its expressiveness, denied its finitude and in a sense its humaneness and so on."[8] His secure sense of himself and his own humanity depended on his conceptual mastery of the environment, and instead of being in command of the attribution of meaning to literalist objects, he felt co-opted by them.

For Fried, this specter of terrifying possibility emanated from the literalist object and infected the self. Material things are haunted, it seemed to say, and so, therefore, are you. As Emily Dickinson put it, "Ourself behind ourself concealed—Should startle most."[9] Seizing hold of the material in an attempt to banish the immaterial—the endlessly possible, that is, or the possibly alien—serves instead to bring it into being. It is an exorcism that conjures what it abhors. Unlike Fried, I would contend that the art of materiality is more, not less, interesting

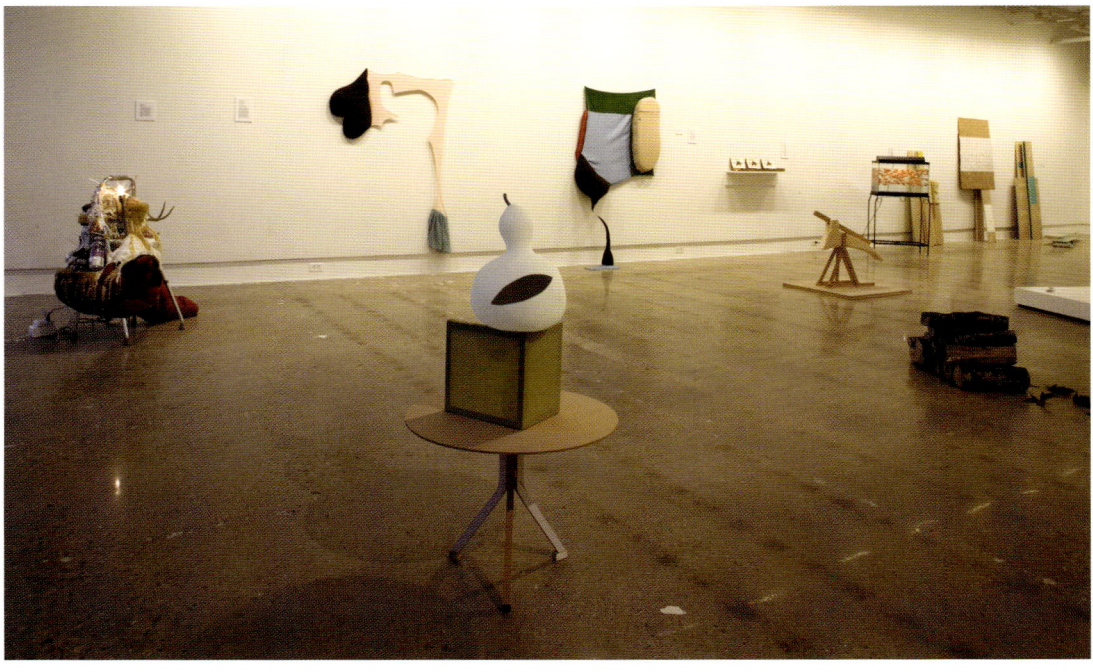

Helen Altman
Harvester 11, detail, 2007
Cigar boxes, color laser print on primed
foil and paper, cast plaster, glue
Edition of 3, 9 x 5½ x 1½" each

Opposite: Chris Sauter
Tower II, 2008
Wheat and glue
36 x 10 x 36"

for its revelation of the immaterial phantasms that we and the world's objects are subject to. Introducing friction into the worldly processes of circulation is more compelling and philosophically useful than smoothing the way.

1 Donald Judd, "Specific Objects," in *Donald Judd, Complete Writings 1959-1975* (Halifax: Nova Scotia College of Art and Design, 2005), 189.
2 Ibid.
3 Ibid.
4 "Don Judd: An interview with John Coplans," in *Don Judd* (Pasadena: Pasadena Art Museum, 1971), 32.
5 Donald Judd, "Lee Bontecou," in *Donald Judd: Complete Writings 1959-1975*, 178.
6 Donald Judd, "Black, White and Gray," in *Donald Judd: Complete Writings 1959-1975*, 117.
7 Jean-Paul Sartre, *La Nausée* (Paris: Gallimard, 1938).
8 Michael Fried, *Art and Objecthood: Essays and Reviews* (Chicago and London: Chicago University Press, 1998), 42.
9 Emily Dickinson, *Selected Poems* (London: Phoenix, 2002) Fascicle 17, Poem 670, 66.

AUTHOR'S BIOGRAPHY

Kirstie Skinner is an art historian based in Scotland. She is currently completing her doctoral research on minimalism and installation art at Edinburgh College of Art, where she was also a lecturer for several years. Published essays include "Moving in the Image" (in Henry Moore Institute and Ashgate's forthcoming volume, *Sculpture and Film*), "Griselda Pollock" (*Art: Key Contemporary Thinkers*, Berg Publishing, 2007), "Camera Perspective" (*Dispatch 114*, Norwich Art Gallery, 2005), "The Picture and the Step" (*Jan De Cock: Denkmal ISBN 9080842427*, Atelier Jan de Cock, 2005), and "The self as a screen" (*Journal for Visual Art Practice*, 3:1, 2004).

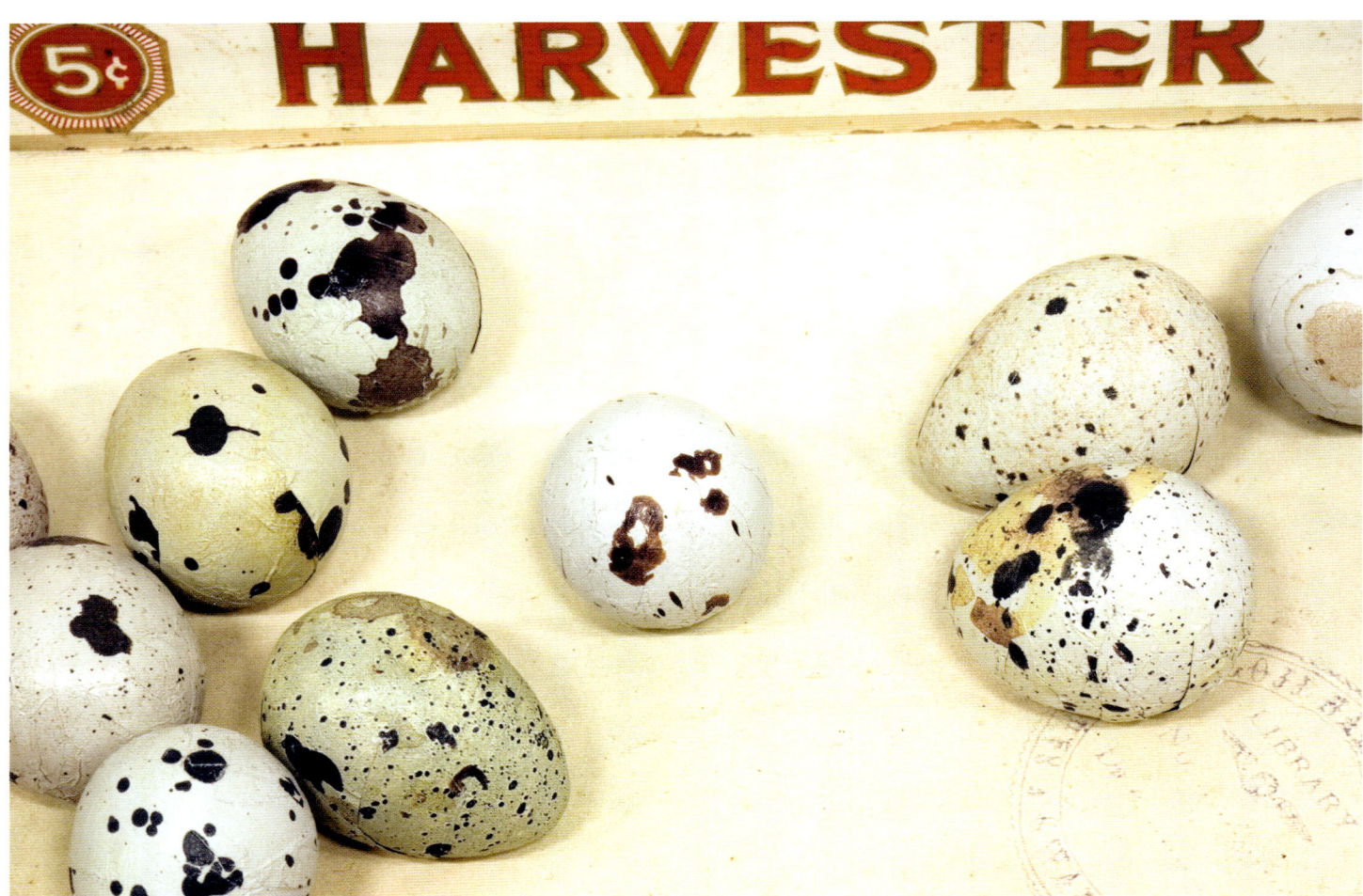

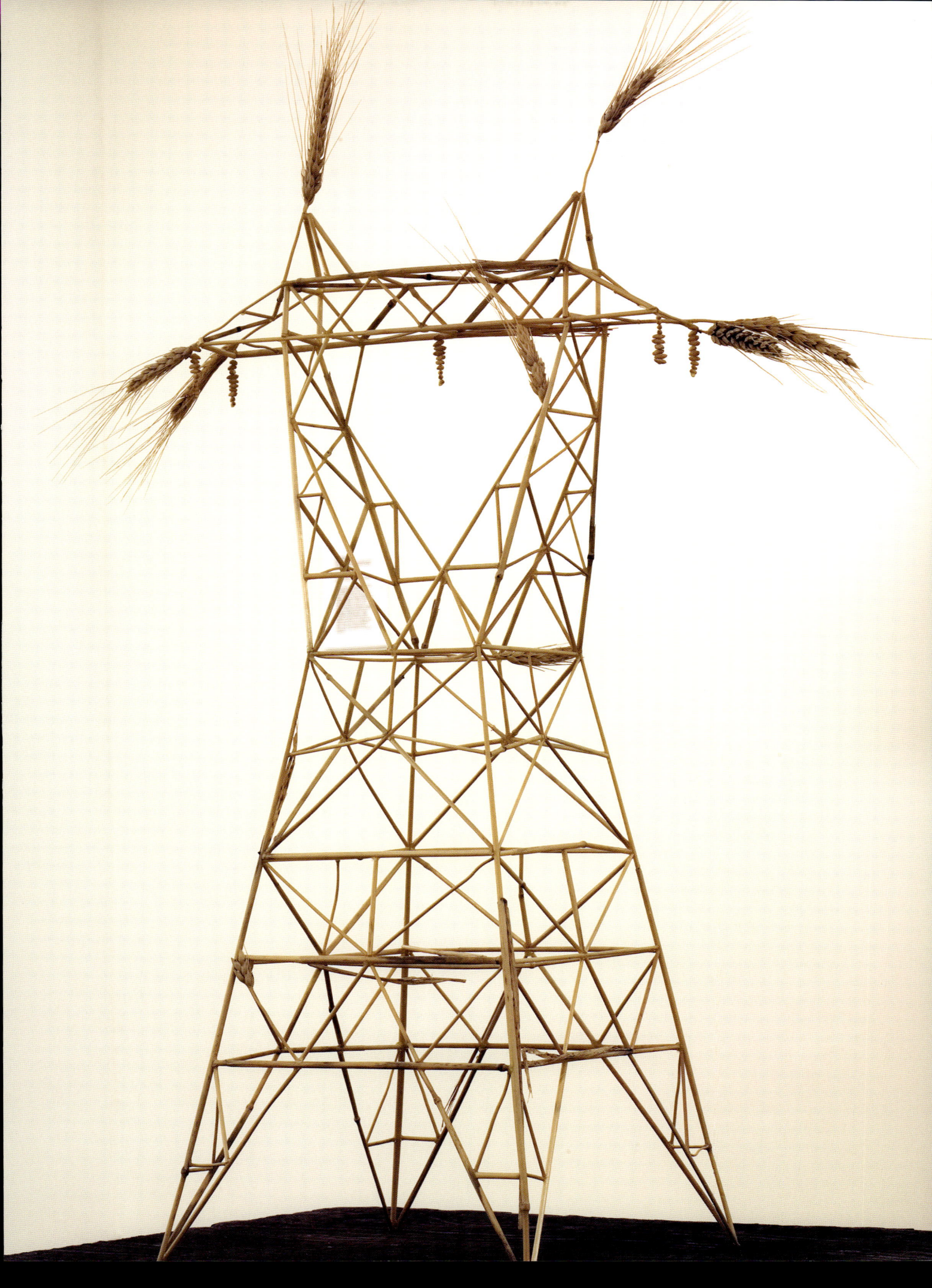

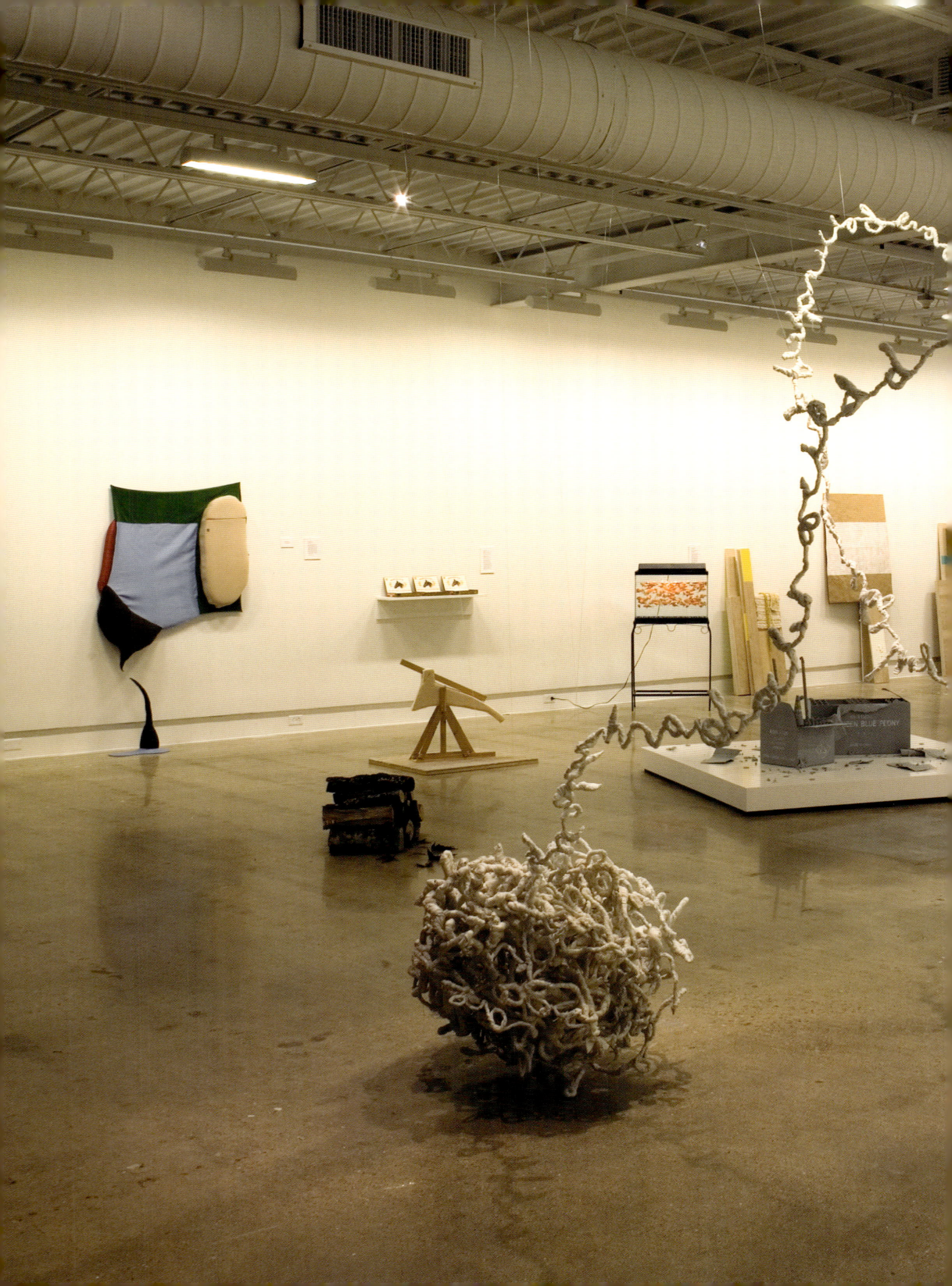

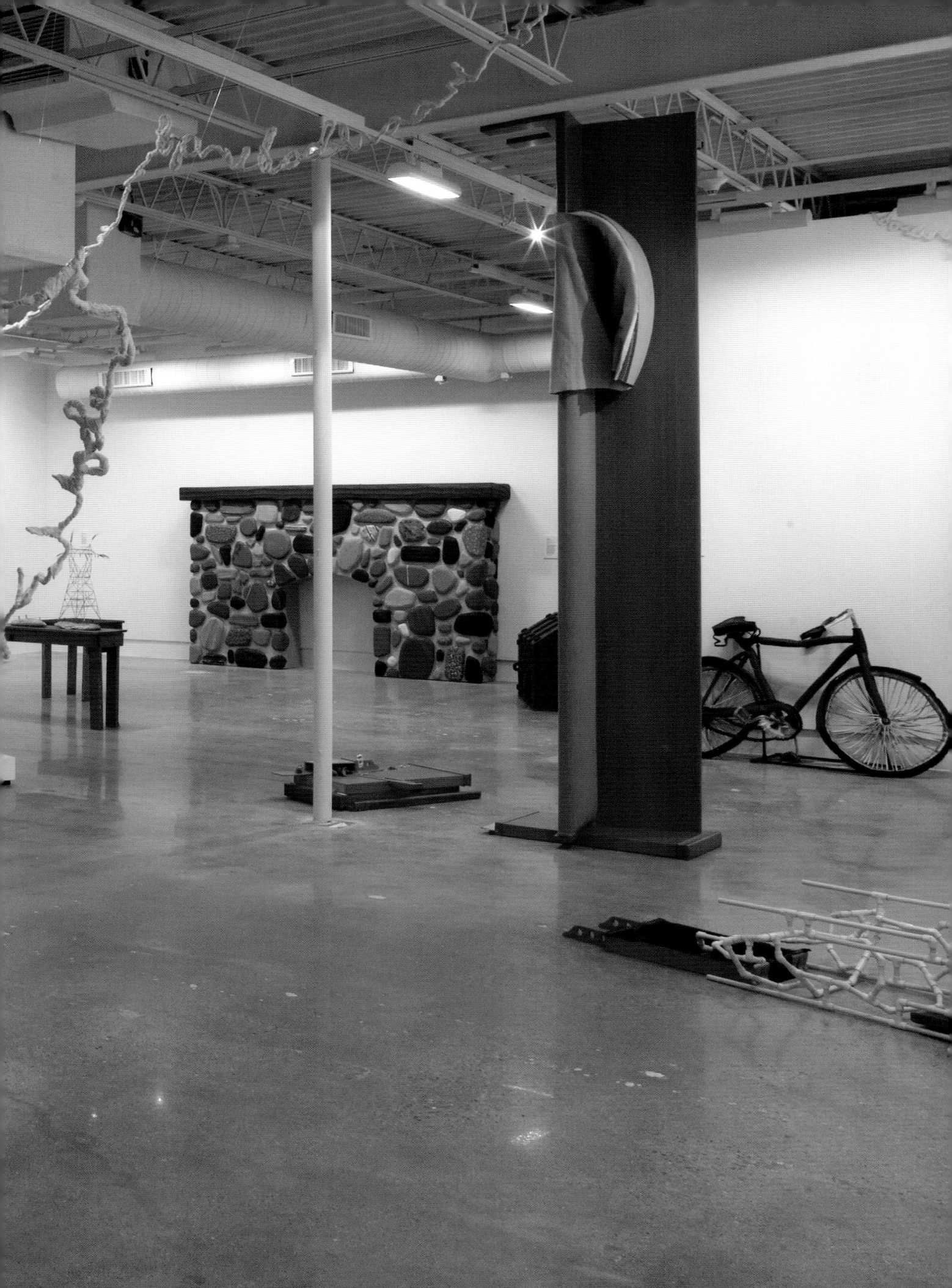

Frankenstein's Madonna: Living In A (Im)Material World by Jennifer Davy

I collected the instruments of life around me, that I might infuse a spark of being into the lifeless thing that lay at my feet.—Mary Shelley, *Frankenstein*

On the eve of the Industrial Revolution one romantic character sought to create life anew out of the detritus of lived life. Possessing "the capacity of bestowing animation,"[1] Victor Frankenstein, Shelley's infamous protagonist, came to life as the modern day Prometheus. Seduced by his own intelligence and equipped with materials garnered from charnel houses, dissecting rooms, and slaughter houses, young Frankenstein set out to recreate existence. Making material the immaterial was typically a production of the religious domain, not of the mortal. Unlike Christianity's Madonna, Frankenstein's conception was his material sin—man's vanity incarnated—and hence his spiritual death. In contrast, today such vanity is more often than not a material asset, the more "you"—the more new and improved "you"—the better. Pop-culture's "touched" virgin, Madonna, has capitalized on such rejuvenating aspects of narcissism since her "original" incarnation in the 1980s. Less prophetic than mimetic, Madonna materialized over the airwaves with a societal soundtrack epitomizing the ubiquity of our material (re)condition.

As Karl Marx underscored the presupposition of Greek art to Greek mythology and its aftereffects as an enduring model of idealism and its subsequent unattainability, one can decidedly underscore the inextricable link between the Industrial Revolution and Marcel Duchamp's revolutionary readymades and their aftereffect as an enduring model of material production and its subsequent insatiability.[2] From a Marxist perspective, the readymade exists because there is the readymade man, like Frankenstein's "creature" cum "wretch," like Madonna "living in a material world." Frankenstein's modern technology—materialized man—exceeded Frankenstein's romantic morality. As such, Frankenstein's ideal became his engendered folly, the master's dark double (among other things), besieged in a tragic descent towards expulsion. While material production deceived Frankenstein it conceived Madonna. She has as yet to exceed herself, as Madonna and her alter ego(s) rely and thrive on excess itself as the very source of redemption and regeneration.

Excess, while in vast supply, has the peculiar ability to perpetually elicit demand. Whether it is expended in the form of luxury or violence, excess, as developed in Georges Bataille's theory of general economy in *The Accursed Share*, is always and already waste albeit a necessary expenditure. The readymades quite clearly epitomize this concept. In particular, Duchamp's *Fountain* (1917)—as an object, as an objet d'art, as a text—objectifies Bataillean excess. It remains a model in contemporary art practice, almost a century past, in part because it has exceeded its own objectification. Beyond the ingenuity of the manufactured object, in the midst of the material wasteland of post-industrial society, such appearances of excess seem blatantly redundant and ironically superfluous. Yet, as excess never ceases to exist nor ceases to provide the artist with material perhaps it is a necessary expense.

Today the "materially inclined" artist is faced with a replenishing gulf to mine. For the artist there is not only the superabundance of production to contend with, but the consequent manufacturing of meaning that the material object has come to represent. It is such excess, both material and immaterial, that in actuality becomes the medium at work in Isa Genzken's sculptural conglomerations. She culls her materials from both the high and low commodity wasteland and sets to work putting their residual effects into play. From masquerade to mutilation Genzken's objects are subjected to and exploited in calculated acts of neutered violence. Whether utilizing a mass-produced synthetic doll or an original Mies van der Rohe Barcelona chair, the artist stages power plays, trauma scenes, and tragic confrontations that seek to emulate the "material conditions" embodied in the objects themselves. Such anthropomorphizing of materials/objects, widely present in contemporary art practices, emerges in and as a very different theatre than that staged by Michael Fried forty years ago in his notorious essay, "Art and Objecthood."

Genzken came of age in the aftermath of such pronouncements. The late 1960s saw material concerns divisively played out from pop art to land art. Lucy Lippard's infamous declaration of the "dematerialization" of the art object, materialized by conceptual art, ushered in a long-standing critique calling into question minimalism's "objecthood" as well as the materiality of art as a commodity in general. While the succeeding decades have evidenced the persistence of the material object in art it has certainly been at the expense of "objecthood," further underscored by such shifting tendencies and strategies as exhibited in Harald Szeemann's *When Attitudes Become Form* at the Kunsthalle in Bern and MoMA's *Information* show in which meaning became the material.

The object becomes much like a pawn moving from objecthood to conditions of display, the latter of which still remains a dominant form today. Haim Steinbach's work is the ideal span accommodating displays of serial commodities upon his signature minimalist inspired triangular shelves. Strategically complicit, the artist's object-based grammar engages all levels of material production from the formal to the fetishistic. Furthering such engagements, Mike Kelley's performative installations tend to develop more from the inert potential levied onto objects than on the objects per se, and thus on the eventuality of such a fabricated mystique. Often through the used and abused, the artist stages the underlying failure of the enculturated object in ceremonial defiance to the material ideal as an attempt to rupture embedded material hierarchies.

Since the 1960s the persistent divestment of physicality, of the thing-in-itself, has been met with an increasing investment in the contingency and agency of the material production of meaning. In material based work, it is never merely the object at hand, but what is in addition to the object at hand; it is the additive "immaterial" that evolves to carry the weight of the work or what Roland Barthes referred to as the "Text" in his essay "From Work to Text." Such movements, from work to text, from the symbolic[3] to the metonymic, develop as effective strategies for materially invested artists as diverse as Jessica Stockholder and Yinka Shonibare. In the latter's work it is precisely the material itself—Dutch Wax—that communicates the artist's post-colonial critique as it is a contingent agent. In its varying manifestations, Victorian costumes, for instance, history, identity, and economy are woven into the very fabric as well as the sculptural object molded by it. In Stockholder's installations the artist compiles assorted garbage and found materials so that "there is a kind of building or layering of meaning that results from the literary content of the objects."[4] Meaning is never given, structured, or narrative, rather it is provoked through the tangential associations of detritus that are as precarious and ephemeral as the material forms they construct.

The growing instability of materiality itself, most poetically realized in the disappearing stacks of Felix Gonzalez-Torres, is as well coincident with the growing sense of the immaterial as championed in the 1985 exhibition *Les Immateriaux* at the Centre de Georges Pompidou. Co-produced with Jean-Francois Lyotard, the exhibition, standing on the shoulders of Marshall McLuhan's ideas, the technology-inspired experiments of the 1960s, and the rise of video and performance as viable media, sought to showcase the material production of the "immaterial" and the pivotal role it was to play in contemporary art and society. While physical objects of art were not in evidence, the exhibition, to be sure, was not simply a mark of material obsolescence but rather a mark of material omnipresence although perhaps in less "concrete" manifestations. Through paraphrasing Lyotard in his essay, "Materiality of Communication," literary theorist K. Ludwig Pfeiffer marks this point of excess whereby "instead of substantial their meanings, we get information overload and a new hardness of 'supporting' materials, a new 'performativity' of things and bodies."[5] Speaking to the cultural effects of "computerized society" such commentary parallels the conditional aesthetics of abundance that have developed in contemporary art.[6]

That the material object is in itself less substantial merely follows physics and the "physics" of a late-capitalist, disposable society; that the more substantial "immaterial" functions as both a repository and a bursary is a residual effect of *the gross cultural landscape*. Thomas Hirschhorn's displays appear to operate precisely within these dynamics, compressing and collapsing the varying temporal states of an object, in which, as Benjamin Buchloh has cited, "the rush from production in a third-world country to distribution in the first, and from the production exchange-value to a brief performance of use-value and imminent dismissal as detritus in ever-decreasing temporal cycles, seems to have become the universal condition of the commodity Hirschhorn's artistic practice mimetically follows."[7]

From critical resistance to critical mimesis (as resistance perhaps), such states of affairs are, and have been, variously played out in what still constitutes sculptural practice from the social sculpture of Joseph Beuys, to the ephemeral collections of Laurie Parsons, to Ai Weiwei's monumental junkyards. Ideally this does not signal a recycling impasse but rather a regenerating *passage* upon a vast expanding and collapsing field of meaning. For the late Jason Rhoades, the latter was true; his oeuvre is an entr'acte. The artist negotiated culture through its materials; his sprawling installations take on epic profundity while at the same time remaining tacit material stuff. His work is littered with abundant and empty referents that always seem to defy semiotic gravity. Untethered, everything and *everything* is set in motion, moving from one thing to the next, from one place to the next, yet never availing a point of departure or arrival.

If there is an issue for the "materialist" it is just that, surplus inertia. For the materially inclined artist in particular, it is not dematerialization, commodification, fetishization, digitization or any of the claims of being in advanced states of such conditions, rather materiality is always already a surfeit. It is the material and the immaterial; it is much like "the fabric of the rhizome," it is "the conjunction, 'and … and … and …'"[8] that the artist, as well as the spectator, must contend with.

1 Mary Shelley, *Frankenstein* (New York: Bantam Books, 1981), 42.

2 Karl Marx, *Grundisse: Foundations of the Critique of Political Economy (Rough Draft)*, trans. Martin Nicolaus (Harmondsworth: Penguin, 1973); cited in *Art In Theory 1815-1900*, ed. Charles Harrison and Paul Wood with Jason Gaiger (Oxford: Blackwell Publishers Ltd, 1998), 341 – 43.

3 Barthes does refer to the symbolic text but distinguishes between a work being moderately symbolic (at best) as opposed to a text being radically symbolic which entails more than (including conception, perception, reception) what is garnered in the general currency of the word symbolic, Roland Barthes, "From Work to Text," in *Image, Music, Text* (New York: Hill and Wang, 1977; Noonday Press edition, 1998).

4 Jessica Stockholder, "In Conversation with Lynne Tilman," *Jessica Stockholder* (London: Phaidon Press, 1995), 34.

5 Pfeiffer uses this quote as an example in his pending argument on the continued reliance on the semantic method of interpretation.

6 In a more superficial sense this parallel acknowledges the currency of the various stylistic terms that have developed over the past few decades (all with roots in the 1960s) and their referential inclinations: appropriation art, context art, institutional critique, scatter art, clusterfuck aesthetics, relational aesthetics, etc.

7 Benjamin Buchloh, "Cargo and Cult: The Displays of Thomas Hirschorn" *Artforum* 40 (November 2001): 173.

8 Gilles Deleuze and Felix Guattari. "Introduction: Rhizome," in *A Thousand Plateaus* (Minneapolis: University of Minnesota Press 1987), 25.

Joseph Havel
Drinks are boiling. Iced drinks are boiling, 2007
Wire, fabric, monofilament
Dimensions variable

AUTHOR'S BIOGRAPHY
Jennifer Davy is an artist and arts writer currently working on her dissertation in the media studies program at the European Graduate School. She received her BFA from the San Francisco Art Institute in Interdisciplinary Studio and her MA from the University of Texas at San Antonio in Art History and Criticism under the direction of Dr. Frances Colpitt.

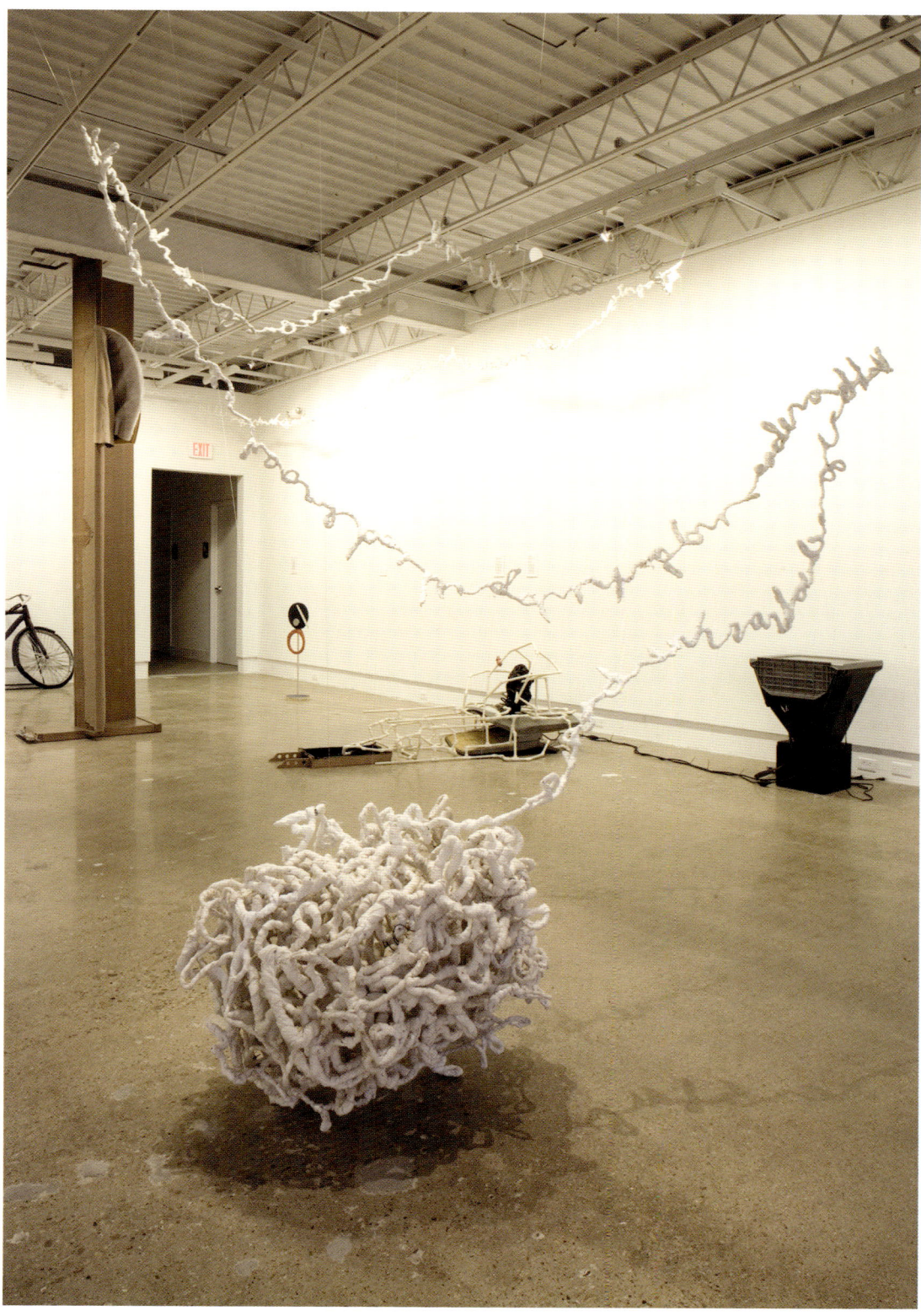

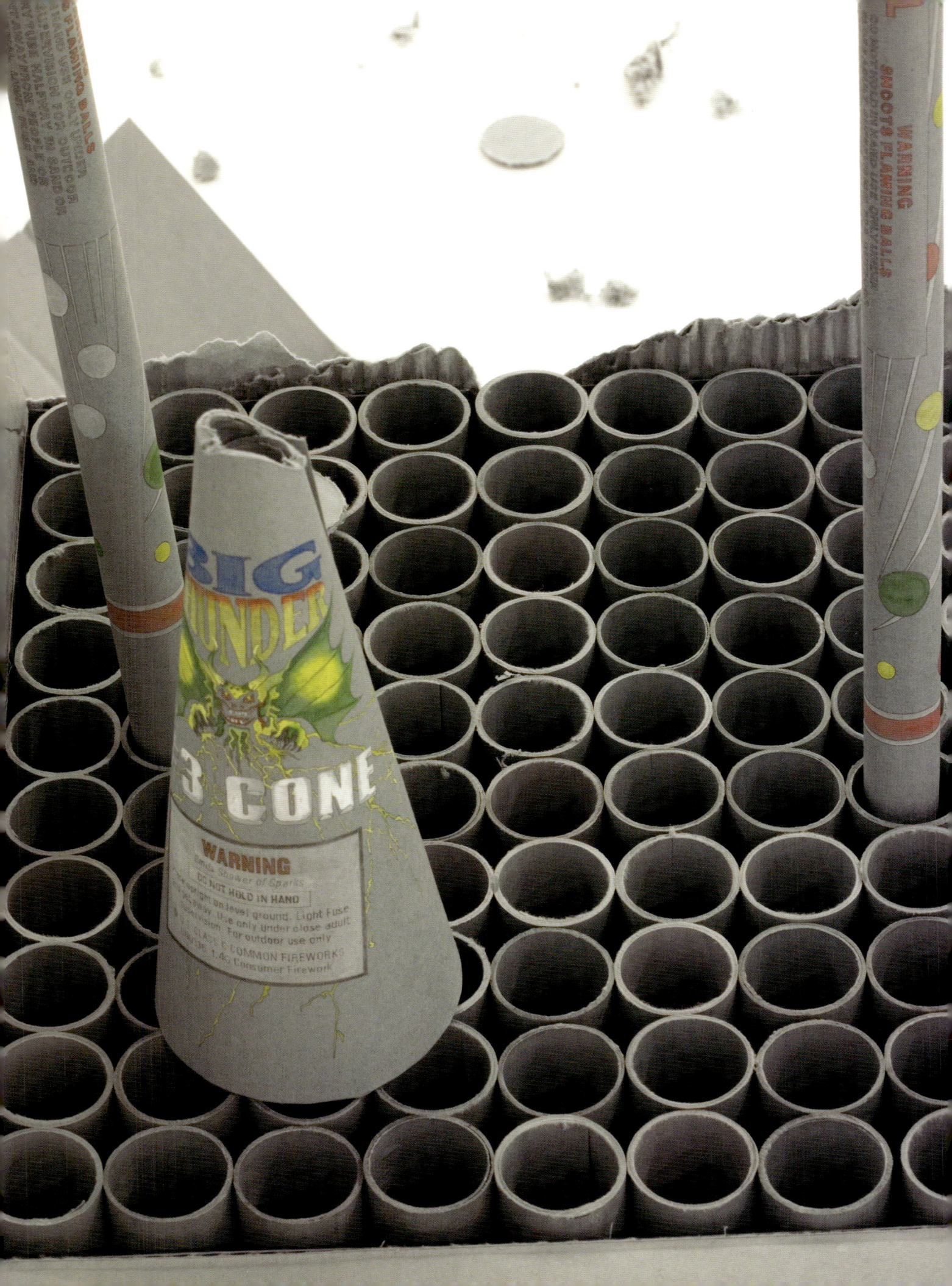

CHECKLIST

Helen Altman
Feeder Tank/The Gathering Storm, 2008
Aquarium, stand and light, water, cast plastic, epoxy, lead weights, monofilament line, 49 x 25 x 13"
Courtesy Dunn and Brown Contemporary, Dallas, and Moody Gallery, Houston

Helen Altman
Harvester 11, 2007
Cigar boxes, color laser print on primed foil and paper, cast plaster, glue
Edition of 3, 9 x 5½ x 1½" each
Courtesy Dunn and Brown Contemporary, Dallas, and Moody Gallery, Houston

Richie Budd
Master Fifty Beef, 2007
Mixed media, 24 x 40 x 38"
Courtesy the artist

Margarita Cabrera
Bicicleta Morada (Purple), 2006
Vinyl, foam, string, wire, 47 x 74 x 30"
Courtesy Sara Meltzer Gallery, New York

Margarita Cabrera
Bicicleta Negra (Black), 2006
Vinyl, foam, string, wire, 47 x 74 x 30"
Courtesy Sara Meltzer Gallery, New York

Bill Davenport
Fireplace, 2007
Papier mâché, 72 x 121 x 13"
Courtesy the artist and Inman Gallery, Houston

Bill Davenport
Treasure Chest, 2006
Styrofoam insulation board and latex house paint, 36 x 48 x 60"
Courtesy the artist and Inman Gallery, Houston

Jonathan Durham
God-shaped Vacuum, 2006
PVC, protoplast, cinema seats, water pump, hymnal, shelves, timer, mineral oil, single channel DVD, television, player, wall mount, dimensions variable
Courtesy the artist

Jonathan Durham
Greater Zion, 2008
Reconstituted church pew, tin, plastic, epoxy, tobacco, 122 x 24 x 34"
Courtesy the artist

Jessica Halonen
Rx Garden (Log pile), 2008
Encaustic on wood, 15 x 26 x 16"
Courtesy the artist

Jessica Halonen
Untitled (defoliated), 2008
Steel and rust, 7 elements, approximately 4 x 5 x 1½" each
Courtesy the artist

Lily Hanson
Phil's Form, 2007
Fabric, foam, wood, wire, 28 x 25 x 5"
Courtesy And/Or Gallery, Dallas

Lily Hanson
She Came a Long Way for Nothing, 2005
Fabric, foam, pins, 65 x 4 x 4"
Courtesy the artist

Lily Hanson
Spindrift Island, 2005
Fabric, foam, cardboard, 68 x 46 x 24"
Courtesy the artist

Joseph Havel
Drinks are boiling. Iced drinks are boiling, 2007
Wire, fabric, monofilament, dimensions variable
Courtesy Dunn and Brown Contemporary, Dallas

Polly Lanning Sparrow
Poulan (Redux), 2008
Latex paint on birch plywood with wool, 54 x 24 x 24"
Courtesy the artist

Polly Lanning Sparrow
Untitled (Blue Configuration), 2008
Latex paint on birch plywood with masking tape, 60 x 66 x 36"
Courtesy the artist

Polly Lanning Sparrow
Untitled (White Configuration), 2008
Kraft paper from leaf and lawn bag, acrylic, oil, birch plywood, 75 x 34 x 12"
Courtesy the artist

Katrina Moorhead
Draumalandid, RedGreenBluePeony, 2007
Archival blue board, archival paper, wheat starch paste, gouache, 60 x 60 x 30"
Courtesy the artist and Inman Gallery, Houston

Chris Sauter
Bread, 2006
Etched copper, thread, ciabatta bread, 4 x 7 x 12" each
Courtesy the artist and Finesilver Gallery, Houston

Chris Sauter
Tower II, 2008
Wheat and glue, 36 x 10 x 36"
Courtesy the artist and Finesilver Gallery, Houston

Brad Tucker
Bumper, 2007
Foam rubber, 15 x 15 x 8"
Courtesy the artist and Inman Gallery, Houston

Brad Tucker
Moon Gourd , 2007
Acrylic and enamel on gourd and wood and fabric, 50 x 19 x 19"
Courtesy the artist and Inman Gallery, Houston

Brad Tucker
Open Globe, 2007
Fabric, acrylic on wood and aluminum, 13 x 39 x 9"
Courtesy the artist and Inman Gallery, Houston

Opposite
Katrina Moorhead
Draumalandid, RedGreenBluePeony, detail, 2007
Archival blue board, archival paper, wheat starch paste, gouache
60 x 60 x 30"

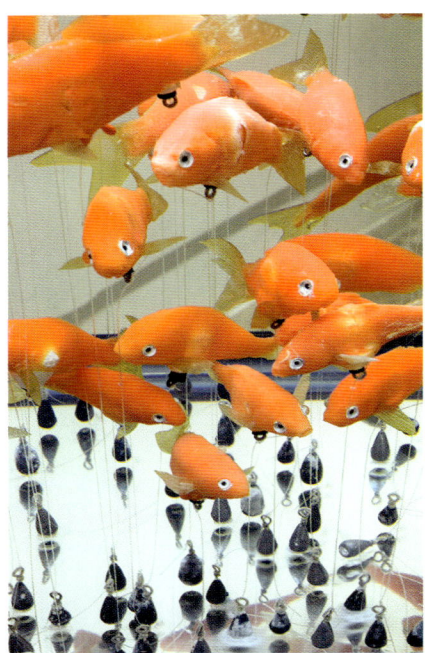

HELEN ALTMAN

Helen Altman (born 1958) holds an MFA degree from the University of North Texas and lives in Fort Worth, where she makes art and has tended to scores of chickens and dogs in her backyard. Crafted to *trompe-l'oeil* perfection, many of her works reveal her love and respect for animals. Her sculptures are folksy, endearingly funny, and deadly serious, without a trace of irony. A variety of materials, including seeds, shaved ice, moving blankets, and even glowing artificial fireplace logs raise life-related issues of birth, growth, and death, characterized by cyclical change and transformation. Her work in *Material Culture* is especially concerned with reproduction by using techniques of photocopying and casting to create multiple identical objects.

EDUCATION

1989 MFA, University of North Texas, Denton, TX
1986 MA, University of Alabama, Tuscaloosa, AL
1981 BFA, University of Alabama, Tuscaloosa, AL

SELECTED INDIVIDUAL EXHIBITIONS

2007 *Floater*, Moody Gallery, Houston, TX
2006, 2004, 2001 *Helen Altman*, Dunn and Brown Contemporary, Dallas, TX
2005 *Scorched*, Carrie Secrist Gallery, Chicago, IL
2004, 2002, 2001 *Helen Altman*, Moody Gallery, Houston, TX
      Patch of Blue, Sarah Moody Gallery of Art, University of Alabama, Tuscaloosa, AL
      Helen Altman: Smoke Signal, DCKT Contemporary, New York, NY
2003 *Helen Altman*, Museum of Contemporary Art, San Diego, CA
2002 *Helen Altman: Fire and Ice*, Glassell School of Art, Museum of Fine Arts, Houston, TX (catalogue)
2001 *Helen Altman: Trailhead*, Women and Their Work, Austin, TX (catalogue)
1999 *Ever Green*, John Michael Kohler Arts Center, Sheboygan, WI (catalogue)
      Running Rabbit, Barry Whistler Gallery, Dallas, TX
1998 *Nature Depicted*, Hiram Butler Gallery, Houston, TX
1997 *Just Ahead*, Art Museum of Southeast Texas, Beaumont, TX (catalogue)
1995 *Ark*, Barry Whistler Gallery, Dallas, TX

SELECTED GROUP EXHIBITIONS

2006 *Photo-based*, Traywick Contemporary, Berkeley, CA
      Furniture as Metaphor: Contemporary Sculpture and the Poetics of Domesticity, University of North Texas Art Gallery, Denton, TX
2005 *Welcome 2 the Jungle*, DCKT Contemporary, New York, NY
      Artists Among Us, The Women's Museum, Dallas, TX
2004 *Art in Embassies Program: Switzerland and Liechtenstein*, United States Embassy, Bern, Switzerland
2003 *Flip*, Dunn and Brown Contemporary, Dallas, TX
2002 *Home Sweet Home*, Arlington Museum of Art, Arlington, TX (catalogue)
2001 *The Inward Eye: Transcendence in Contemporary Art*, Contemporary Arts Museum, Houston, TX (catalogue)
      Burn: Artists Play with Fire, Norton Museum of Art, West Palm Beach, FL; The Columbia Museum of Art, Columbus, SC (catalogue)
2000 *Out of the Ordinary: New Art from Texas*, Contemporary Arts Museum, Houston, TX (catalogue)
      Texas Dialogues: Scenic Overlook, Blue Star Art Space, San Antonio, TX (catalogue)
      Natural Deceits, Modern Art Museum of Fort Worth, Fort Worth, TX (catalogue)
      Small, The Old Jail Art Center, Albany, TX (catalogue)
      Making a Mark: Experimental Drawing and Printmaking, University Art Gallery, Central Michigan University, Mt. Pleasant, MI
1999 *Threshold: Invoking the Domestic in Contemporary Art*, John Michael Kohler Arts Center, Sheboygan, Wisconsin; Contemporary Art Center of Virginia, Virginia Beach, VA (brochure)
1998 *ARTS BOTANICA*, Ida Green Gallery, Austin College, Sherman, TX
1997 *Surface Tensions*, Blue Star Art Space, San Antonio, TX (brochure)
      Schemata: Drawings by Sculptors, Glassell School of Art, Museum of Fine Arts, Houston, TX (catalogue)
1996 *Transformers: A Moving Experience*, Auckland Art Gallery, Auckland, New Zealand; Hiram Butler Gallery, Houston, TX (catalogue)
      Burning Issues, Galveston Art Center, Galveston, TX
1995 *The Home Show*, University of Texas at San Antonio Art Gallery, San Antonio, TX
      Das Pop, Donna Beam Fine Art Gallery, University of Nevada, Las Vegas, NV (brochure)

SELECTED BIBLIOGRAPHY

Colpitt, Frances. "Helen Altman at Barry Whistler," *Art in America* 83 (June 1995).
Goad, Kimberly. "Emerging Artists," *Art & Antiques*, February 2000.
Greene, Alison de Lima. *Texas: 150 Works from the Museum of Fine Arts, Houston*, New York: Harry N. Abrams, 2000.
Johnson, Patricia. "Between Two Worlds," *Houston Chronicle*, 23 November 1993.
_____. *Contemporary Art in Texas*. Roseville East, Australia: Craftsman House, 1995.
_____. "Exhibits Offer Expressive Explorations," *Houston Chronicle*, 27 September 2002.
Kutner, Janet. "Established Artists Steal the Show," *Dallas Morning News*, 29 May 1994.
Ludlam, Jane. "Appliance Angst," *Houston Press*, 4 October 1990.
Mitchell, Charles Dee. "Gallery Enters with Elegance," *Dallas Morning News*, 30 October 2000.
Odom, Michael. "Helen Altman: Dunn and Brown Contemporary," *Artforum* 40 (January 2002).
Ostrower, Jessica. "Helen Altman at DCKT," *Art in America* 92 (September 2004).
Tyson, Janet. "Helen Altman, Matthew Sontheimer, and Liz Ward," *ARTnews* 99 (February 2000).
_____. "A Very Contemporary," *Fort Worth Star Telegram*, 15 December 1996.

Helen Altman
Feeder Tank/The Gathering Storm, detail, 2008
Aquarium, stand and light, water, cast plastic, epoxy, lead weights, monofilament line
49 x 25 x 13"

RICHIE BUDD

A witty *bricoleur*, Richie Budd (born 1975) produces teeming assemblages in which found objects—mostly mass produced consumer items—are cobbled together with hot glue and other inventive fasteners. Kinetic but utterly non-utilitarian, his work is intended to stimulate the five senses and often includes bits of fast food or fragrant drugstore sundries. There is also a dark side in his humorous sculpture's commentary on runaway consumerism. A former member of the Good/Bad Art Collective, based in Denton, Budd received a BFA from UNT and MFA from UTSA. He currently lives in San Antonio and is represented by Priska C. Juschka Fine Art in New York.

EDUCATION

2006 MFA, University of Texas at San Antonio, San Antonio, TX
2000 BFA, University of North Texas, Denton, TX

SELECTED INDIVIDUAL EXHIBITIONS

2007 *Bon Voyage Monstromos De Pileon*, Texas A&M International University Gallery, Laredo, TX
Emoting Skillformational Rememories, Priska Juschka Fineart Gallery, New York, NY
2006 *Helpin' Hand*, permanent installation, Vermont Studio Center, Johnson, VT
Richie Budd, Finesilver Gallery, Houston, TX
What's Going On Behind What's Going On, Tortilleria La Popular, San Antonio, TX
2004 *How Are You Understanding Under It Now?*, Gallery 4, Blue Star Contemporary Art Center, San Antonio, TX
1997 *One-Person Show Featuring Richie Budd*, Good/Bad Art Collective, Denton, TX

SELECTED GROUP EXHIBITIONS

2007 *Triangle Arts Association 25th Anniversary Alumni Art Exhibition*, DUMBO Arts Festival, DUMBO, New York, NY
Waiting to Explode, Lawndale Art Center, Houston, TX
Tabletop Sculpture, Art Palace, Austin, TX
Texas Uprising, University of Texas at San Antonio Art Gallery, San Antonio, TX
Road Agent: The Audience is Listening: Remastering the Original Analog Tapes (with bonus tracks!), Road Agent, Dallas, TX
Object, University of Texas at Dallas, Dallas, TX
2006 *Lowering the Hoop Enough for Everyone*, installation/performance, Open Studios: Vermont Studio Center, Johnson, VT
Insanely Sick, i2i Gallery, San Antonio, TX
Bluestar 21, Blue Star Contemporary Art Center, San Antonio, TX
2005 *Transcendental Damn*, Fresh Up Club, Austin, TX
Siamese Triplets, UTSA Satellite Space, San Antonio, TX
Ulterior Motifs no. 9, Wheeler Brother's Studio, Lubbock, TX
At Home in San Antone', New Braunfels Museum Of Art and Music, New Braunfels, TX
Texas Biennial, City of Austin, Austin, TX
Urbanisms of Risk, University of Texas at Dallas, Dallas, TX
2004 *New Stars/Contemporary Art Month 19*, Finesilver Gallery, San Antonio, TX
Environmental Excursions, Subspace Gallery, Berlin, Germany
1998 *Very Fake, But Real*, DiverseWorks, Houston, TX
Red Rover Issues, Mark Allen's Revolution Summer, Houston, TX
1997 *Video Night 3*, Good/Bad Art Collective, Denton, TX
The Designs of Bob Mackie, Sailors on Shore Leave, 500-X, Dallas, TX
1996 *Microwavable*, Good/Bad Art Collective, Denton, TX
1995 *Discord*, Glassell School of Art, Museum of Fine Arts, Martha Bush Gallery, Houston, TX

SELECTED BIBLIOGRAPHY

Cohen, Rebecca S. "Texas Biennial 2005," *ART LIES*, no. 46 (Spring 2005).
Davenport, Bill. "Castoffs are Art in the Hands of Richie Budd," *Houston Chronicle*, 12 June 2006.
Davis, Ben. "Mess Haul: Richie Budd's Sculptures Cook Popcorn and Meat," *Village Voice*, 5 June 2007.
Gupta, Anjali. "Reviews Nationwide, *Environmental Excursions*," *artUS*, no. 3 (June / August 2004).
Hart Chambers, Christopher. "Grilling Up the Hellhound Rodeo," *dart International* 10 (Fall 2007).
Jankauskas, Jennifer. "Detritus and a Hot Glue Gun: Exploring the Lo-Fi Art Aesthetic," *Glasstire.com: Texas Visual Art Online*, March 2005 (http://live.glasstire.com).
Plocek, Keith. "Good Budd: At Lawndale, It's Popcorn, Boogie Boards and Neuro-linguistic Programming," *Houston Press*, 22 February 2007.
Rees, Christina. "Manhattan Transfer: Denton's Good/Bad Art Collective Takes Its Act to New York And Hopes to Survive the City's Brutal Art," *Dallas Observer*, 29 July 1999.
Schuker, Lauren A. E. "Art for Less," *Wall Street Journal*, 21 July 2007.

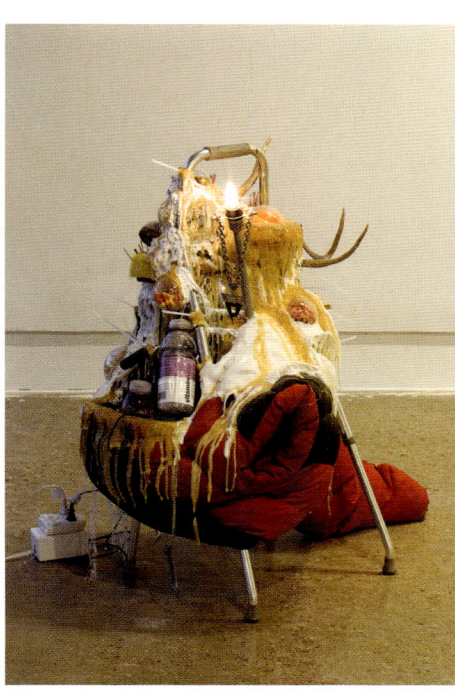

Richie Budd
Master Fifty Beef, 2007
Mixed media
24 x 40 x 38"

MARGARITA CABRERA

A highly recognized young sculptor, Margarita Cabrera (born 1973) was raised in Mexico City and lives in El Paso. She received her BFA and MFA from Hunter College of the City University of New York and has exhibited widely since 2002. In 2007, she was a finalist for the prestigious Texas Prize. Made with hand-sewn fabric or vinyl formed into the shape of commonplace, mass-produced objects (or, in other instances, the ubiquitous cactus), her sculptures typically investigate U.S./Mexico tensions due to migrant labor and exploitation by the maquiladoras. Her soft, lifesize bicycles, recalling the work of Claes Oldenburg, represent a common form of transportation around and across the border.

EDUCATION

2001 MFA, Hunter College of the City University of New York, New York, NY
1997 BFA, Hunter College of the City University of New York, New York, NY
Maryland Institute College of Art, Baltimore, Maryland

SELECTED INDIVIDUAL EXHIBITIONS

2008 *New Works 08.1: The Craft of Resistance*, Artpace San Antonio, International Artist-in-Residence Program, San Antonio, TX (catalogue)
2007 *Margarita Cabrera*, Walter Maciel Gallery, Los Angeles, CA
2006, 2004, 2003 *Margarita Cabrera*, Sara Meltzer Gallery, New York, NY
2005 Adair Margo Gallery, El Paso, TX
2004 *VOCHO*, Women and Their Work, Austin, TX
2002 *Dynamic Peripheries*, Plan b Center for Contemporary Art, Santa Fe, NM
1999 *Cazenovia*, Cazenovia College, Cazenovia, NY

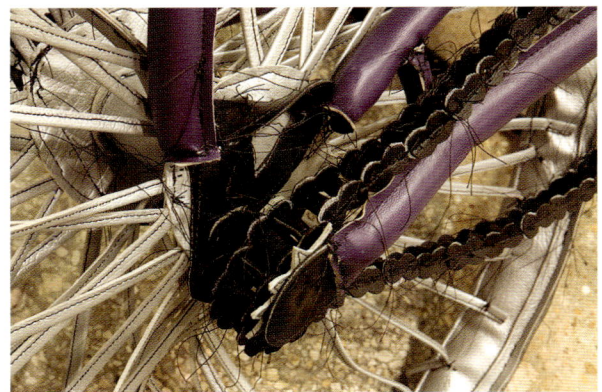

SELECTED GROUP EXHIBITIONS

2008 *Margarita Cabrera, Ali Smith, and Willie Cole*, Finesilver Gallery, Houston, TX
Phantom Sightings: Art After the Chicano Movement, Los Angeles County Museum of Art, Los Angeles, CA (catalogue)
2007 *Arthouse Texas Prize 2007*, Arthouse at the Jones Center, Austin, TX (catalogue)
Sonatube, Santa Barbara Contemporary Arts Forum, Santa Barbara, CA
The Border in Painting, Sculpture, and Photography, Adair Margo Gallery, El Paso, TX
Margarita Cabrera and Billy Hassell, The Gallery at UTA, Arlington, TX
2006 *Explorations, Explorations*, Edward Cella + Architecture (ECAA), Santa Barbara, CA
Macy's Window Project, Macy's, New York, NY
Moved by the Machine: Art Inspired by the Automobile, Dubuque Museum of Art, Dubuque, IA
Welcome Home, Sara Meltzer Gallery, New York, NY
As Good As Your Next Gig, Walter Maciel Gallery, Los Angeles, CA
2005 *Take Shape*, Rena Bransten Gallery, San Francisco, CA
Rearranged/Redefined: Domestic Objects Reconsidered, Mainline Art Center, Philadelphia, PA
2004 *Domicile: A Sense of Place*, Center on Contemporary Art, Seattle, WA
Twang: Contemporary Sculpture From Texas, Art Museum of Southeast Texas, Beaumont, TX; McKinney Avenue Contemporary, Dallas, TX (catalogue)
Domestic Odyssey, San Jose Museum of Art, San Jose, CA (catalogue)
Borderlands, El Paso Museum of Art, El Paso, TX
2003 *Blanc*, Mexican Institute of Culture, Washington, D.C.; Design District, Miami, FL
CORPORAL: Contemporary Women Artists from Latin America, Schmidt Gallery, Florida Atlantic University, Boca Raton, FL
2002 *The S-Files*, El Museo Del Barrio, New York, NY (catalogue)
2001 *Two to Tango*, Times Square Gallery, New York, NY
2000 *Weight as Real*, House Gallery, Long Island City, NY
1999 *War, Artist Bulletin Board*, Postmasters, New York, NY
1998 *Par Avion*, Hunter College, New York, NY
RKS, Groningen, Holland
1997 *Young Artists Exhibition*, New World Art Center, New York, NY

SELECTED BIBLIOGRAPHY

Aranca, Rocio. "Margarita Cabrera," *Art Nexus 2* (December 2003 / February 2004).
Aukeman, Anastasia. "Margarita Cabrera at Sara Meltzer," *Art in America* 95 (January 2007).
Buckley, Annie. "Margarita Cabrera," *Artillery* 1 (May 2007).
Cotter, Holland. "Critical Consumption," *New York Times*, 7 March 2004.
____. "The S Files," *New York Times*, 17 January 2003.
Hymes, Sarah. "Margarita Cabrera and Billy Hassell at the Gallery at UTA," *Glasstire: Texas Visual Arts Online*, February 2007 (http://live.glasstire.com).
Kley, Elisabeth, "Margarita Cabrera: Sara Meltzer," *ARTnews* 104 (March 2005).
Rosenberg, Karen. "Show and Tell: Margarita Cabrera," *New York Times Magazine*, 8 May 2006.
Schulze, Troy. "The Eyes of Texas: Lone Star Artists are a Breed of Their Own," *Houston Press*, 16 – 22 August 2007.
Self, Bernadette Sedillos. "Border Influences Artist to Create Vinyl VW Beetle," *El Paso Times*, 7 September 2004.
Sullivan, James. "A Love Affair with Appliances Only Keeps Us in the Kitchen," *San Francisco Chronicle*, 25 March 2004.

Margarita Cabrera
Bicicleta Morada (Purple), detail, 2006
Vinyl foam, string, wire
47 x 74 x 30"

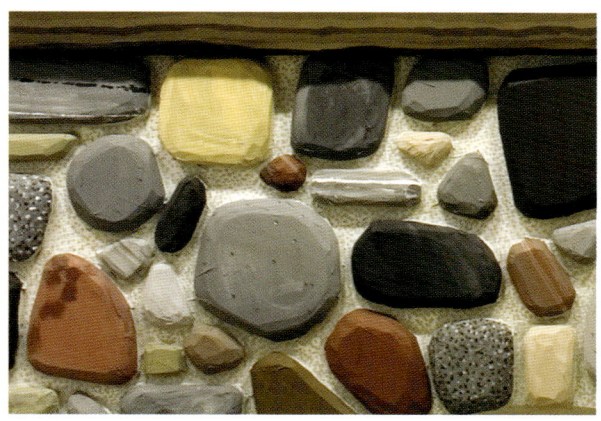

BILL DAVENPORT

Bill Davenport (born 1962) has lived in Houston since 1990, when he was awarded a Core Fellowship at the Glassell School of Art, Museum of Fine Arts, Houston. He received his MFA from the University of Massachusetts in Amherst and has an extensive record of well received exhibitions, including solo shows in New York, Munich, and throughout Texas. A finalist for the 2007 Texas Prize, Davenport is a powerful influence on younger artists in the state. He is devoted to the *craft* of object-making, utilizing a variety of processes such as casting, crocheting, carving, clay modeling and glazing, thrift-store assemblage, and *faux* architectural detailing. His sculptures conjure the pretense and illusion associated with Disneyland and Hollywood movies with gleeful complicity.

EDUCATION
1990 MFA, University of Massachusetts, Amherst, MA
1986 BFA, Rhode Island School of Design, Providence, RI

SELECTED INDIVIDUAL EXHIBITIONS
2006, 2004, 1999, 1994 *Bill Davenport*, Inman Gallery, Houston, TX
2003 *Slow Birds*, Angstrom Gallery, Dallas, TX
2001 *Spectaculess*, Homeroom, Munich, Germany
1998 *1998/1999 Crash*, Sala Diaz, San Antonio, TX
1997 *Art with Cats*, Good/Bad Art Collective, Denton, TX
      One Man and a Van, Cristinerose Gallery, New York, NY
1993 *Equivalents to the Real World*, Wierbowski Gallery, Houston, TX
1990 *Contemporary Readymades: Selected and Arranged Sculpture by Bill Davenport*, Student Union Gallery, University of Massachusetts, Amherst, MA

SELECTED GROUP EXHIBITIONS
2007 *Arthouse Texas Prize 2007*, Arthouse at the Jones Center, Austin, TX (catalogue)
      Book Works, Galveston Arts Center, Galveston, TX
2006 *The Searchers,* White Box, New York, NY
2005 *New Texas Painting*, DiverseWorks, Houston, TX
      Bill Davenport, Francesca Fuchs, Brad Tucker, Ibid Projects, London, England
      Conversational Lag, Volume Gallery, New York, NY
2004 *Brothers*, The Fresh Up Club, Austin, TX
      I Heart Texas, Allston Skirt Gallery, Boston, MA
      Books and Shelves, Gahlberg Gallery, College of Du Page, Glen Ellyn, IL
      Twang: Contemporary Sculpture From Texas, Art Museum of Southeast Texas, Beaumont, TX; McKinney Avenue Contemporary, Dallas, TX (catalogue)
2003 *Family Circus*, Clementine Gallery, New York, NY
      Patterns and Serial Randomness, Beaker Gallery, Tampa, FL
      Collage/Joining, Devin Borden Hiram Butler Gallery, Houston, TX
      Slab, University Galleries, Illinois State University, Normal, IL (catalogue)

2002 *Blip*, University of South Florida Contemporary Art Museum, Tampa, FL
      Hard Core, Galveston Arts Center, Galveston, TX
2001 *The New Orleans Triennial*, New Orleans Museum of Art, New Orleans, LA (catalogue)
      Bang, Barbara Davis Gallery, Houston, TX
      PAN, Czech Centre, London, England
2000 *Thrifting*, Lombard-Freid Fine Art, New York, NY
      Natural Deceits, Modern Art Museum of Fort Worth, Fort Worth, TX (catalogue)
      Neo-Rococo, University of Texas at San Antonio Art Gallery, San Antonio, TX
1999 *Size Matters*, Gale Gates et al., Brooklyn, NY
      By Design, Contemporary Art Collective, Las Vegas, NV
      Hot Spots, Weatherspoon Art Gallery, University of North Carolina, Greensboro, NC
1998 *The Texas Show*, ABC No Rio, New York, NY
      Nirvana, British Council Window Gallery, Prague, Czech Republic
      Blunt Object, Smart Museum of Art, University of Chicago, Chicago, IL
1997 *Thread*, Cristinerose Gallery, New York, NY
      Women's Work, Arlington Museum of Art, Arlington, TX (catalogue)
1996 *Buttered Side Up,* Hallwalls Contemporary Arts Center, Buffalo, NY
      The Big Show, Lawndale Art and Performance Center, Houston, TX
1995 *Continental Discourse: Art of Mexico and the United States Today*, San Antonio Museum of Art, San Antonio, TX (catalogue)
      Analogs of Modernism, McKinney Avenue Contemporary, Dallas, TX (catalogue)
1994 *Faith in Doubt*, University at Buffalo Art Gallery/Research Center in Art + Culture, Buffalo, NY (catalogue)
1992 *1992 Core Artists in Residence Exhibition*, Glassell School of Art, Museum of Fine Arts, Houston, TX (catalogue)
1991 *1991 Core Artists in Residence Exhibition*, Glassell School of Art, Museum of Fine Arts, Houston, TX (catalogue)

SELECTED BIBLIOGRAPHY
Allen, Mark. "Buttered Side Up," ART LIES, no. 4 (December/January 1994).
Allen, Wren M. "Bill Davenport, Francesca Fuchs and Brad Tucker; IBID Projects," ART LIES, no. 49 (Winter 2006).
Bourbon, Matthew. "Bill Davenport: Slow Birds," ART LIES, no. 38 (Spring 2003).
Colpitt, Frances. "Bill Davenport at Inman," Art in America 84 (March 1996).
_____. "Space City Takes Off," Art in America 88 (October 2000).
_____. "Southern Sensibilities," Art in America 89 (November 2001).
Hess, Jean. "Disiptoey ('Strategies for Abstraction')," Art Papers 21 (September/October 1997).
Kalil, Susie. "The Small and The Dreadful," Houston Press, 17 – 23 November 1994.
Kutner, Janet. "Three Texas Abstractionists Strut Their Stuff," Dallas Morning News, 12 April 1996.
Lunde, Paige. "Albee's Seescape: Interview with Edward Albee," ART LIES, no.4 (Spring 1997).
Moody, Tom. "Bill Davenport," Artforum 35 (April 1997).
Odom, Michael. "Bill Davenport: Angstrom Gallery," Artforum 38 (October 1999).
_____. "Forth Worth: Natural Deceits," Art Papers 24 (November/December 2000).
Schaffner, Ingrid. "Thread," Artforum 36 (February 1998).
Smith, Mary Katherine. "Bill Davenport," ART LIES, no. 9 (October/November 1995).
Tyson, Janet. "A Toast to Abstract Art," Fort Worth Star Telegram, 12 April 1996.

Bill Davenport
Fireplace, 2007
Papier mâché
72 x 121 x 13"

JONATHAN DURHAM

Minute and fragile connections between objects and ideas drive the construction of the quirky, highly idiosyncratic sculptures of Jonathan Durham (born 1975). In his dense assemblages, heavily symbolic found objects are dismembered, reconstructed, refashioned, or obscured. Often, three-dimensional mazes of PVC create a closed, impenetrable, yet strangely figurative circuit. His work alludes to surveillance and viewing situations, the frightening implications of military activities, and in the case of *Greater Zion* the power of organized religion. Durham grew up in Virginia, where, he said, his "family was very involved in a protestant church." He received an MFA from UCLA in 2000. From 2005 – 07, he was a Core Fellow at the Glassell School of Art, Museum of Fine Arts in Houston. Durham lives and works in Houston and New York.

EDUCATION

2000 MFA, University of California, Los Angeles, Los Angeles, CA
1997 BA, University of Virginia, Charlottesville, VA

SELECTED INDIVIDUAL EXHIBITIONS

2006 *Where Is Thy Sting?: New Sculpture and Video*, Lawndale Art Center, Houston, TX
2004 *Cyrus (The Younger) / Zero Degree Monumentality*, Old Nature Gallery, Charlottesville, VA
      New Sculpture & Video, Fayerweather Gallery, Charlottesville, VA

SELECTED GROUP EXHIBITIONS

2007 *New American Talent,* Arthouse at the Jones Center, Austin, TX
      2007 Core Artist in Residence Exhibition, The Glassell School of Art, Museum of Fine Arts, Houston, TX (catalogue)
2006 *2006 Core Artist in Residence Exhibition*, The Glassell School of Art, Museum of Fine Arts, Houston, TX (catalogue)
      Drawing/Inside Out, Lawndale Art Center, Houston, TX
2004 *Lucky 13*, ADA Gallery, Richmond, VA
2003 *Last Tango*, Fayerweather Gallery, Charlottesville, VA
2002 *Faculty Exhibition*, Cerritos College, Norwalk, CA
2001 *Library Project*, Galerie FurGenwaartskunst, Bremen, Germany
2000 *MFA Group Show*, UCLA Wight Gallery, Los Angeles, CA
1999 *This Guy* (collaborative performance with Erin Cosgrove), UCLA Warner Studios, Los Angeles, CA

SELECTED BIBLIOGRAPHY

Bhatnagar, Priya. "Husks of Men," *2007 Core Artists in Residence Exhibition*. Houston: Museum of Fine Arts, 2007.
Klaasmeyer, Kelly. "Core Artists-in-Residence Exhibition," *Houston Press*, 5 April 2007.

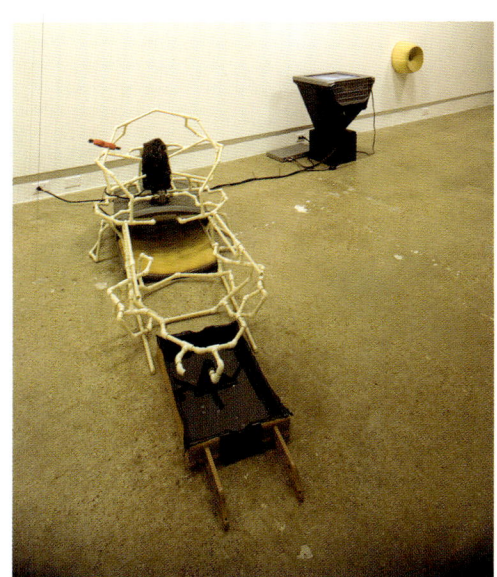

Jonathan Durham
God-shaped Vacuum, 2006
PVC, protoplast, cinema seats, water pump, hymnal, shelves, timer, mineral oil, single channel DVD, television, player, wall mount
Dimensions variable

JESSICA HALONEN

Jessica Halonen (born 1972) was a Core Fellow at the Glassell School of Art, Museum of Fine Arts, Houston, in 2000 – 01. She currently lives in Austin and teaches at Trinity University in San Antonio. An inventive sculptor, Halonen creates enigmatic installations that derive from biological and ecological concerns. Her inspirations range from personal medical conditions (reflected in her use of bar graphs) to larger issues such as the interaction of nature and artifice. Recently, her work has utilized both living trees and wooden logs. Like many contemporary artists, she uses any materials—from found objects to traditional art supplies—that suit the work's concept, resulting in the avoidance of a personal "style."

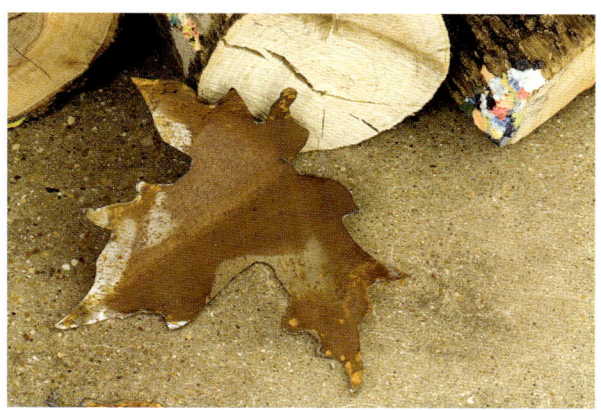

EDUCATION

1999 MFA, Washington University, St. Louis, MO
1994 BA, Kalamazoo College, Kalamazoo, MI
       Universidad de Extremadura, Caceres, Spain

SELECTED INDIVIDUAL EXHIBITIONS

2006 *Zone 3 to 7*, Garden Project, Dallas Center for Contemporary Art, Dallas, TX
2004 *Picnic Baskets*, Window Works Project, ArtPace: A Foundation for Contemporary Art/San Antonio, TX
       Scattered, Women and Their Work, Austin, TX
2003 *Still*, Trinity University, San Antonio, TX
       Picnic, UTSA Satellite Space, San Antonio, TX
2000 *A Satisfying Arrangement*, Maxwell Freeman Contemporary Pictures, Houston, TX

SELECTED GROUP EXHIBITIONS

2007 *PLOT*, Jessica Halonen and Emily Joyce, Park Projects, Los Angeles
       Drawing: New Accessions to the Permanent Collection, Museum of Fine Arts, Houston, TX
       High Five: Emerging Art in America, CW Channel Corporation Headquarters, Los Angeles, CA (catalogue)
2006 *I-35*, Dunn and Brown Contemporary, Dallas, TX
       From/About, Keki Gallery, Budapest, Hungary
2005 *Rock, Paper, Scissors*, Arlington Museum of Art, Arlington, TX (catalogue)
       Southern Space Project, San Antonio, TX
       Blue Star 20, Blue Star Art Space, San Antonio, TX
       Trickle Down 'Invisible Attraction,' Firehouse Center for the Visual Arts, Burlington, VT
       Gardens Real and Imagined, Austin Museum of Art, Austin, TX (catalogue)
2004 *Draw_drawing*, Gallery 32, London, England
       Piros Szoba Gallery, Balatonfüred, Hungary
       Twang: Contemporary Sculpture From Texas, Art Museum of Southeast Texas, Beaumont, TX; McKinney Avenue Contemporary, Dallas, TX (catalogue)
2002 *Building Blocks*, Dallas Center for Contemporary Art, Dallas, TX (brochure)
2001 *Floored*, University of Texas at Dallas, Dallas; University of Dallas, Irving, TX
       Colorfast, Houston Community College, Houston, TX
       Black Air: New Film and Video from Houston, Aurora Picture Show, Houston, TX
       2001 Core Artists in Residence Exhibition, Glassell School of Art, Museum of Fine Arts, Houston, TX (catalogue)
       COLORFORMS, Lawndale Art Center, Houston, TX
       Daze, University of Texas at Dallas, Dallas, TX
2000 *The Big Show*, Lawndale Art Center, Houston, TX
       Sculpture 2000: Site/Works, Chenevert Green, Houston, TX
       2000 Core Artists in Residence Exhibition, Glassell School of Art, Museum of Fine Arts, Houston, TX (catalogue)
1999 *Merged Realities*, Central Arts Coalition, Tucson, AZ
1997 *Art Saint Louis XIII*, St. Louis Design Center, St. Louis, MO
1995 *New Work: Jessica Halonen & Eric Conrad*, Jaszkasino, Jaszbereney, Hungary

SELECTED BIBLIOGRAPHY

Cohen, Rebecca. "Jessica Halonen, Scattered," *ART LIES*, no. 43 (Summer 2004).
Colpitt, Frances. "Space City Takes Off," *Art in America* 88 (October 2000).
Daniel, Mike. "'Daze' at UT-Dallas," *Dallas Morning News*, 26 January 2001.
"Jessica Halonen, Wobble," *San Antonio Current*, 15 – 22 July 2004.
Mitchell, Charles Dee. "Accent Not Included," *Dallas Morning News*, 19 March 2005.
Pearson, Christopher. "Visions in Plaid: Jessica Halonen's Picnic," *ART LIES*, no. 39 (Summer 2003).
Schutze, Jim. "Sculpture o' the South," *Dallas Observer*, 24 February – 2 March 2005.
Velliquette, Michael. "Jessica Halonen: Picnic," *Glasstire: Texas Visual Arts Online*, May 2003 (http://live.glasstire.com).
Wing, Carlin. "Jessica Halonen and Emily Joyce: PLOT at Park Projects," *...might be good*, no. 84, 23 February 2007 (http://www.fluentcollab.org).

Jessica Halonen
Rx Garden (Log pile), detail, 2008
Encaustic on wood
15 x 26 x 16"

Untitled (defoliated), detail, 2008
Steel and rust
7 elements approximately 4 x 5 x 1½" each

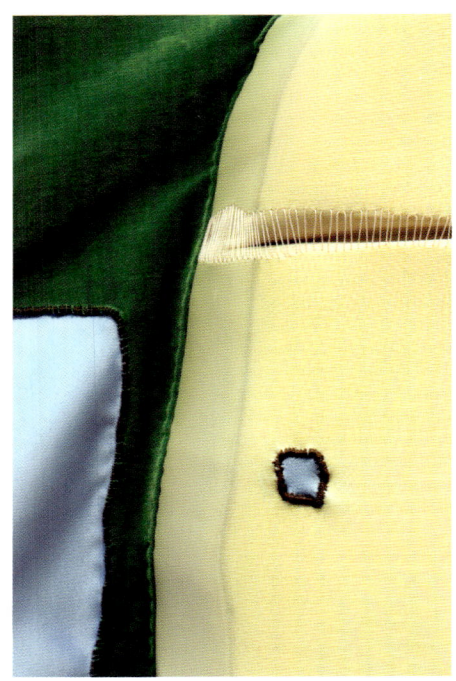

LILY HANSON

Working primarily with soft, stretchy fabric over foam rubber supports, Lily Hanson (born 1971) creates quirky constructions that refer to, without representing, the human body. They not only mimic the scale, bulges, and curves of the body but the way in which clothing sheathes the flesh. Hanson is especially admired for her bold use of color and careful craftsmanship, which include tiny, perfectly identical stitches, an even spacing of staples holding the fabric, and gently puckered seams that exude a subtle tension. With an MFA from SMU, Hanson participated in the University of Texas at Dallas' Southside residency program in 2005. She lives and works in Dallas, where her work has begun to attract critical attention.

EDUCATION

2000 MFA, Southern Methodist University, Dallas, TX
1995 BA, Hampshire College, Amherst, MA

SELECTED INDIVIDUAL EXHIBITIONS

2007 *Would You Be Mine?* (collaboration with David Willburn), 500X Gallery, Dallas, TX
      Object, University of Dallas, Dallas, TX
2006 *Lily Hanson*, Mountain View College, Dallas, TX
2005 *Lily & Mrs. Mohamaddi go on a Sea Voyage*, Eastfield College, Mesquite, TX

SELECTED GROUP EXHIBITIONS

2007 *Differentia*, Lawndale Arts Center, Houston, TX
      Contexture: Fabric, Fashion, and Fantasy, Space 301, Mobile, AL
      Show #10: Lily Hanson + Jason Singleton, And/Or Gallery, Dallas, TX
      Texas Biennial, Dougherty Arts Center, City of Austin, Austin, TX
2005 *Double Vision*, The Old Jail Art Center, Albany, TX
      Lily Hanson & Son Doo Kim, Janette Kennedy Gallery, Southside on Lamar, Dallas, TX
      Space-Invaders, University of Texas at Dallas, Dallas, TX; Eugene Binder, Marfa, TX
      Gimme Shelter, Conduit Gallery, Dallas, TX
      Open Studios, Shamrock Hotel Studios, Dallas, TX
2004 *Eastfield College Faculty Exhibition*, Eastfield College, Mesquite, TX
      Twang: Contemporary Sculpture From Texas, Art Museum of Southeast Texas, Beaumont, TX; McKinney Avenue Contemporary, Dallas, TX (catalogue)
      Skin, Conduit Gallery, Dallas, TX
2001 *Feisty*, 500X Gallery, Dallas, TX
      19th Annual Art in the Metroplex, TCU Art Gallery, Fort Worth, TX
      Episodes, Conduit Gallery, Dallas, TX
      Texas National 2001, Stephan F. Austin University, Nacogdoches, TX
      Ulterior, Haggerty Gallery, University of Dallas, Irving, TX
      Expo 2000, 500X Gallery, Dallas, TX
2000 *Suspect Idols*, Cactus Bra Gallery, San Antonio, TX
      New Texas Talent 2000, Craighead-Green Gallery, Dallas, TX
      Prison/Dormitory/Dayroom (collaboration with James Casebere), McKinney Avenue Contemporary, Dallas, TX
      Master of Fine Arts Qualifying Exhibition, Pollock Gallery, Southern Methodist University, Dallas, TX
1999 *A Fresh Look at Texas Art*, McKinney Avenue Contemporary, Dallas, TX
      Fourteen, 500X Gallery, Dallas, TX
1997 *Manifest*, Copley Society of Artists, Boston, MA
1995 *Installation*, Vermont Studio Center, Johnson, VT
      Division III Exhibition, Hampshire College, Amherst, MA

SELECTED BIBLIOGRAPHY

McCabe, Bret, "Natural Wonders," *Dallas Observer*, 22 – 28 March 2001.
Rees, Christina. "Consider the Copycat," *Dallas Observer*, 11 – 17 January 2001.
Simblist, Noah. "Why Have There Been No Great Women Artists?" *Glasstire: Texas Visual Arts Online*, May 2006 (http://live.glasstire.com).
Terranova, Charissa. "Gimmie Shelter," *Glasstire: Texas Visual Arts Online*, August 2005 (http://live.glasstire.com).
_____. "Lily Hanson, Mistress of the Soft and Uncanny," *Glasstire: Texas Visual Arts Online*, January 2007 (http://live.glasstire.com).
Zotos, John. "Episodes," *ART LIES*, no. 32 (Fall 2001).

Lily Hanson
She Came a Long Way for Nothing, 2005
Fabric, foam, pins
65 x 4 x 4"

JOSEPH HAVEL

Joseph Havel (born 1954) is an internationally recognized sculptor based in Houston and the Director of the Glassell School of Art and its Core Program. Havel's early work was based on the transformation or reproduction of found objects such as curtains, lampshades, and men's white dress shirts. These gendered, domestic objects allowed him to explore feminist issues along with the sculptor's traditional concern with the body. For *Drinks are boiling. Iced drinks are boiling*, Havel wrapped wire with strips of torn white bed sheets before shaping the wire into the fluid words of a poem by John Berryman, "Dream Song #46." While the text is strung throughout the gallery, barely legible shadows of the words appear on the adjacent walls.

EDUCATION
1979 MFA, Pennsylvania State University, University Park, PA
1975 BFA, University of Minnesota, Minneapolis, MN

SELECTED INDIVIDUAL EXHIBITIONS
2007 *Joseph Havel: New Castle*, Baltic Centre for Contemporary Art, Gateshead, England
2006 *Joseph Havel: Drinks are boiling. Iced drinks are boiling*, Laumeier Sculpture Park, St. Louis, MO (catalogue)
  Joseph Havel: A Decade of Sculpture 1996 – 2006, Museum of Fine Arts, Houston, TX (catalogue)
2006, 2004, 2003, 2001 *Joseph Havel*, Dunn and Brown Contemporary, Dallas, TX
2005, 2003, 2001, 2000, 1998, 1995 *Joseph Havel*, Devin Borden Hiram Butler Gallery, Houston, TX
2004 *Lost/Lust*, ARCO, Madrid, Spain with Devin Borden Hiram Butler Gallery, Houston, TX
2003 *Le Jeu Du Travailleur*, Galerie Gabrielle Maubrie, Paris, France
2002 *Desire*, Palais de Tokyo, Paris, France
2001 *Daydream Nation*, Galerie Gabrielle Maubrie, Paris, France
1999 *Joseph Havel, Lost: Shirt Labels, Nothing Photographs, Dream Drawings*, Galveston Art Center, Galveston, TX
1997 *Joseph Havel: Commun*, Galerie Gabrielle Maubrie, Paris, France (catalogue)
  Joseph Havel, INOVA (Institute of Visual Arts), Milwaukee Art Museum, University of Wisconsin, Milwaukee, WI
  Joseph Havel, Center for Curatorial Studies, Bard College, Annandale-on-Hudson, NY
1996 *Joseph Havel*, Huntington Beach Art Center, Huntington Beach, CA (catalogue)
  Joseph Havel, Soros Center for Contemporary Art, Kiev, Ukraine

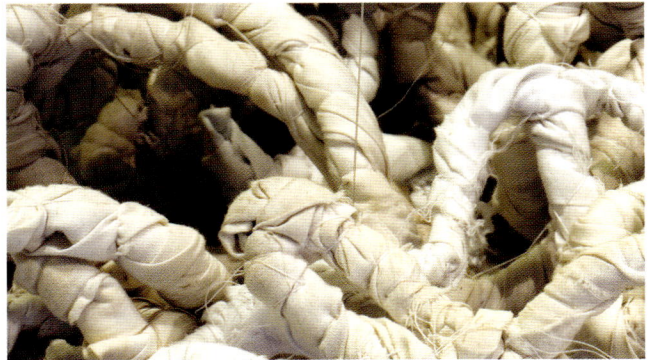

SELECTED GROUP EXHIBITIONS
2007 *Gaspar Enriquez and Joseph Havel*, The Gallery at UTA, University of Texas at Arlington, TX
2006 *Furniture as Metaphor: Contemporary Sculpture and the Poetics of Domesticity*, University of North Texas Art Gallery, Denton, TX
2005 *Texas Vision: The Barrett Collection*, Meadows Museum of Fine Art, Dallas, TX
2004 *Borderlands: Images, Objects & Identity*, El Paso Museum of Art, El Paso, TX
  5 Years of S.M.A.K., Stedelijk Musaeum voor Actuele Kunst, Ghent, Belgium
  Whiteness, A Wayward Construction, University of Virginia Museum, Charlottesville, VA; Laguna Art Museum, Laguna Beach, CA (catalogue)
  Sculpture from the Art in Embassies Program, Department of State, Washington, D.C.
  Joseph Havel/Richard Serra: Works on Paper, Devin Borden Hiram Butler Gallery, Houston, TX
2003 *Basel Art Fair*, Galerie Gabrielle Maubrie, Paris, France
  Contemporary Texas Artists in France, Art in Embassies Program, U.S. Embassy, Paris, France
2002 *110 Years: The Permanent Collection at the Modern Art Museum of Fort Worth*, Modern Art Museum of Fort Worth, Fort Worth, TX (catalogue)
2001 *The Draftsman's Colors: Fourteen New Acquisitions from Johns to Chong*, Whitney Museum of American Art, New York, NY
  Space: Sculptors' Drawings About Sculpture, Museum of Fine Arts, Houston, TX
2000 *Whitney Biennial of American Art*, Whitney Museum of American Art, New York, NY (catalogue)
1999 *Street Life*, Project Row Houses, Houston, TX
  On the Ball: The Sphere in Contemporary Sculpture, DeCordova Museum and Sculpture Park, Lincoln, MA
1998 *Interactions: Mark Gomes, Joseph Havel, Lisa Ludwig, Susan Schelle*, Freedman Gallery, Center for the Arts, Albright College, Reading, PA; Centre Contemeporaranea Borges Buenos Aires, Argentina (catalogue)
  Tenth Anniversary, Contemporary Museum, Honolulu, HI
1997 *Landscape: The Pastoral to the Urban*, Center for Curatorial Studies Museum, Bard College, Annandale-on-Hudson, NY
  American Images: The SBC Collection of Twentieth-Century American Art, Museum of Fine Art, Houston, TX; Austin Museum of Art, Austin, TX (catalogue)
1996 *Shirts and Skins: Absence/Presence in Contemporary Art*, Contemporary Art Museum, Contemporary Art Museum, Honolulu, HI
  Three Visions, El Centro Cultural Borges, Buenos Aires, Argentina
1995 *Twentieth-Century American Sculpture at the White House*, The First Lady's Garden, Washington, D.C.
  Das Pop, Donna Beam Fine Art Gallery, The University of Nevada, Las Vegas, NV

SELECTED BIBLIOGRAPHY
Aukeman, Anastasia. "Shopping: Deitch Projects," *ARTnews* 96 (January 1997).
Doroshenko, Peter. "Joseph Havel in Conversation with Peter Doroshenko," *ART LIES*, no. 7 (June/July 1995).
Ennis, Michael. "Joseph Havel, Breaking the Mold," *Texas Monthly*, September 2000.
Greene, Alison de Lima. *Texas: 150 Works from the Museum of Fine Arts, Houston* (New York: Harry N. Abrams, 2000).
Lightman, Victoria. "Joseph Havel," *Sculpture* 16 (September 1997).
Montgomery, Robert. "Joseph Havel: Baltic," *Modern Painters* 19 (June 2007).
Myers, Holly. "White Noise, Where Race Meets the Sand, Laguna Beach," *LA Weekly*, 25 April – 1 May 2003.
Odom, Michael. "Joseph Havel," *Artforum* 45 (May/June 2006).
Sans, Jérôme. "Review: Joseph Havel," *Art Press*, no. 231 (January 1998).
_____ and Marc Sanchez. *Tokyobook* 2. Paris: Palais de Tokyo, 2001.
Tyson, Janet. "The 2000 Whitney Biennial: An Interview with Michael Auping," *ART LIES*, no. 25 (Winter 1999 – 2000).
Vogel, Carol. "Surprises in the Whitney's Biennial Selections," *New York Times*, 8 December 1999.

Joseph Havel
Drinks are boiling. Iced drinks are boiling, 2007
Wine, fabric, monofilament
Dimensions variable

KATRINA MOORHEAD

Winner of the 2007 Texas Prize, Katrina Moorhead (born 1971) is a native of Northern Ireland, educated at Edinburgh College of Art, and a resident of Houston where she was a Core Fellow at the Glassell School of Art, Museum of Fine Arts, Houston (1996 – 98). Distinguished by a light and delicate sensibility and a focus on the overlooked, her work is quietly unassuming but infinitely rewarding, given careful inspection of its tiniest details. It is frequently inspired by personal experiences that are transformed into collective memories. Like other artists in this exhibition, she is highly dependent on her hands and fingers, imparting a human touch to inert materials. *Draumalandid ...* represents a box of exploded fireworks (encountered on a recent residency in Iceland) created entirely from folded and glued sheets of archival blue paper.

EDUCATION

1996 MFA, Edinburgh College of Art/Heriot-Watt University, Edinburgh, Scotland
1994 BA, Edinburgh College of Art/Heriot-Watt University, Edinburgh, Scotland

SELECTED INDIVIDUAL EXHIBITIONS

2007 *a thing called early blur*, Blaffer Gallery, The Art Museum of the University of Houston, Houston, TX (catalogue)
   Katrina Moorhead, James Harris Gallery, Seattle, WA
2006 *a pretty girl that this man does not love her*, Inman Gallery, Houston, TX
2005 *New Works 05.3: an island as it might be*, ArtPace: A Foundation for Contemporary Art/San Antonio, International Artist in Residence Program, San Antonio, TX (catalogue)
2004 *Ideal Total Now*, Devin Borden Hiram Butler Gallery, Houston, TX
   Stutter, Project Room, Blue Star Art Space, San Antonio, TX
1998 *Katrina Moorhead*, Devin Borden Hiram Butler Gallery, Houston, TX
1997 *Katrina Moorhead*, Lynn Goode Gallery, Houston, TX

SELECTED GROUP EXHIBITIONS

2008 *We Construct The Chorus*, iSpace, University of Illinois Urbana-Champaign, Chicago, IL
2007 *Texas Prize 2007*, Arthouse at the Jones Center, Austin, TX (catalogue)
2006 *Texas 100: Selections from the El Paso Museum of Art*, El Paso Museum of Art, El Paso, TX
   Sparkle, Gallery Side 2, Tokyo, Japan
   Architectural Utopias, Art Gallery of Greater Victoria, Victoria, BC, Canada
   Sincerity, Finesilver Gallery, San Antonio, TX
   Xtra-Ordinary: Francesca Fuchs, Thomas Glassford and Katrina Moorhead, Arthouse at the Jones Center, Austin, TX
2005 *The Nature of Things*, Ormeau Baths Gallery, Belfast, Northern Ireland; Istituto Provinciale Per L'Infanzia, Santa Maria della Pieta (catalogue)
   51st Venice Biennale, Venice, Italy (catalogue)
   Things Fall Apart, Monique Meloche Gallery, Chicago, IL
2004 *Sampled Sky*, Billboard Project, Lawndale Art Center, Houston, TX
   Floral Graffiti: The future is empty, easy to convince, and ours (collaboration with Maggie Hills), Vardy Off-Site Projects, The Vardy Gallery, University of Sunderland, Sunderland, England (brochure)
   Twang: Contemporary Sculpture From Texas, Art Museum of Southeast Texas, Beaumont, TX; McKinney Avenue Contemporary, Dallas, TX (catalogue)
   Greyscale/CMYK, in association with the Nordic Institute for Contemporary Art/ Network North, Royal Hibernian Academy, Dublin, Ireland (catalogue)
2002 *New Additions to the Altoids Curiously Strong Collection*, New Museum of Contemporary Art, New York, NY
2001 *Space: Sculptors' Drawings About Sculpture*, Museum of Fine Arts, Houston, TX
   Out of Sorts, Perspectives 2001, Ormeau Baths Gallery, Belfast, Northern Ireland (catalogue)
   Thrifting, Lombard-Freid Fine Arts, New York, NY
   The Munchie Munchie, DiverseWorks, Houston, TX (catalogue)

1999 *Material, Process, Memory*, Jones Center for Contemporary Art, Austin, TX (catalogue)
   Simply Beautiful, Contemporary Arts Museum, Houston, TX (catalogue)
1998 *1998 Core Artists in Residence Exhibition*, Glassell School of Art, Museum of Fine Arts, Houston, TX (catalogue)
1997 *1997 Core Artists in Residence Exhibition*, Glassell School of Art, Museum of Fine Arts, Houston, TX (catalogue)
1996 *Blank Expression*, Art of This Century, Houston, TX
1995 *Karaoke Fluxfest*, Collective Gallery, Edinburgh, Scotland

SELECTED BIBLIOGRAPHY

Bonetta, Francesca. "Northern Ireland at the Venice Biennale," *Circa*, no. 114 (Winter 2005).
Cook, Fachel. "Sin Cera," *ART LIES*, no. 49 (Winter 2006).
French, Christopher. "Katrina Moorhead," *Sculpture* 26 (May 2007).
Lin, Joseph. "Katrina Moorhead: a pretty girl that this man does not love her." *ART LIES*, no. 52 (Fall 2006).
Monseau, Michele. "Katrina Moorhead: *an island as it might be*," *...might be good*, no. 58, 2 December 2005 (http://www.fluentcollab.org).
Threadgill, Brendan. "Katrina Moorhead," *artUS*, no. 21 (January / February 2008).
Van Ryzin, Jeanne Claire. "Arthouse at the Jones Center," *Austin-American Statesman*, 27 February 2004.
White, Michelle. "Katrina Moorhead's Poetic Perceptions," *Art Papers* 30 (May / June 2006).

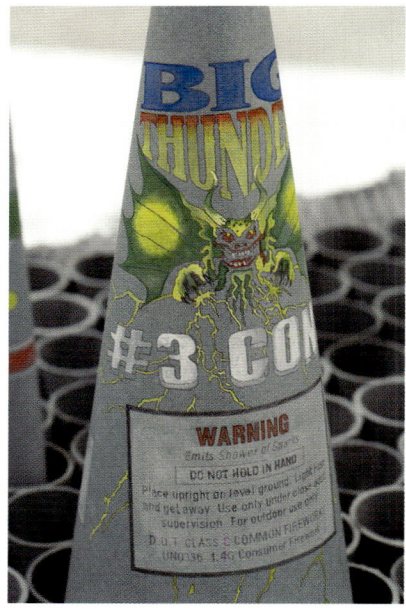

Katrina Moorhead
Draumalandid, RedGreenBluePeony, detail, 2007
Archival blue board, archival paper, wheat starch paste, gouache
60 x 60 x 30"

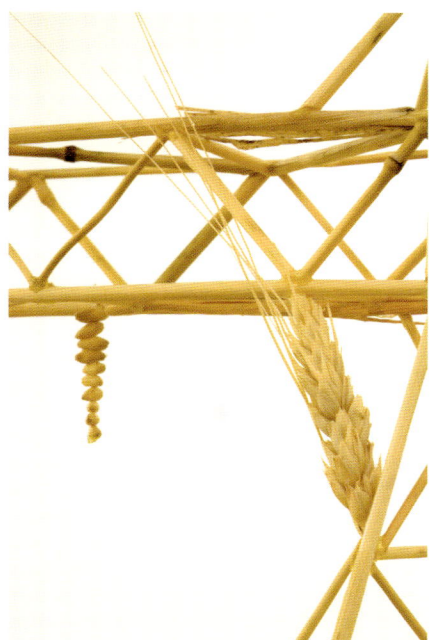

CHRIS SAUTER

A native Texan with an MFA from UTSA, Chris Sauter (born 1971) has an international exhibition record, with solo shows in New York, Paris, Houston, Los Angeles, Chicago, and San Antonio, where he lives and works. In 1999, he participated in the International Artist-in-Residence program at ArtPace, producing a recreation of his family's dining room furniture from the sheet-rocked walls of the gallery in which the work was exhibited. Highly personal, Sauter's work often derives from childhood memories or the shelter of the family home. Exploring a variety of trajectories, ranging from the Texas landscape to sexual identity, he is also a professional baker, and wheat and bread figure prominently in his repertoire of domestic materials.

EDUCATION

1996 MFA, University of Texas at San Antonio, San Antonio, TX
1993 BFA, University of the Incarnate Word, San Antonio, TX

SELECTED INDIVIDUAL EXHIBITIONS

2007 *HomeMaker*, Cueto Project, New York, NY
      Workshop, Finesilver Gallery, Houston, TX
2006 *Pioneer*, Finesilver Gallery, San Antonio, TX
2005 *Power Lines*, Susanne Vielmetter Los Angeles Projects, Culver City, CA
      The Known Universe, FIAC, Galerie Valerie Cueto, Paris, France
      Museum, DiverseWorks, Houston, TX
      Big Bang, Galerie Valerie Cueto, Paris, France
2004 *Just Married*, Elizabeth Dee Gallery, New York, NY
2003 *Gallery*, Art Statements, Art Basel/Miami, Miami Beach, FL
      Planting Eden, TBA Exhibition Space, Chicago, IL
2002 *I'm Just an Old Lump of Coal*, Three Walls, San Antonio, TX
2001 *Light Industry*, Cactus Bra, San Antonio, TX
2000 *Chris Sauter*, Project Room, San Antonio, TX
1999 *New Works 99.3: Graft*, ArtPace: A Foundation for Contemporary Art/
      San Antonio, International Artist in Residence Program, San Antonio, TX
      (catalogue)

SELECTED GROUP EXHIBITIONS

2007 *¿y Que?: Queer Art in Texas*, Landmark Arts, Lubbock, TX
      SouthwestNET: Drawing Outside the Lines, Scottsdale Museum of Contemporary
       Art, Scottsdale, AZ (brochure)
      Cherry Picked: 2007 Survey of Texas Art and Artists, WFMA 40th Anniversary
      Exhibition, Wichita Falls Museum of Art, Wichita Falls, TX
      Zeitgeist, Cueto Project, New York, NY
2006 *That's What I Like About Texas*, Polvo, Chicago, IL
2005 *Wall to Wall Drawing*, Drawing Center, New York, NY (brochure)
      Domicile: Privée/Public, Musée d'Art Moderne de Saint-Etienne Metropole,
      SaintEtienne, France (catalogue)
      Open EV+A, Limerick City Gallery of Art, Limerick, Ireland (catalogue)
2004 *Farm to Market*, ArtPace: A Foundation for Contemporary Art/San Antonio,
      San Antonio, TX
      Drop Out, Julie Saul Gallery, New York, NY
      Deconstruction por un Construction, Galerie Valerie Cueto, Paris, France
      The Sublime is (Still) Now, Elizabeth Dee Gallery, New York, NY
      Twang: Contemporary Sculpture From Texas, Art Museum of Southeast Texas,
      Beaumont, TX; McKinney Avenue Contemporary, Dallas, TX (catalogue)
2003 *Come Forward: Emerging Art in Texas*, Dallas Museum of Art, Dallas, TX
      (catalogue)
      Beyond the Academy: Encouraging New Talent From Texas, Arthouse at the
      Jones Center, Austin, TX (catalogue)
2002 *10x3*, San Antonio Museum of Art, San Antonio, TX
2001 *Once There Was A Spot*, Locust Projects, Miami, FL
      Personal Playgrounds, Austin Museum of Art, Austin, TX
      Cropduster, James Gallery, Houston, TX
2000 *Charles LaBelle, Chris Sauter*, Sala Diaz, San Antonio, TX
      Out of the Ordinary: New Work From Texas, Contemporary Arts Museum,
      Houston, TX (catalogue)
1999 *Temporary Things*, James Gallery, Houston, TX
      Generation Z, P.S.1 Contemporary Art Center, Long Island City, NY
      Phenotypology, Hallwalls Contemporary Arts Center, Buffalo, NY (brochure)
1997 *Space: Architecture + Installation*, Arlington Museum of Art, Arlington, TX
      (catalogue)
      New American Talent, Texas Fine Arts Association, Austin, TX
1996 *Double Trouble: Mirrors, Pairs, Twins, Lovers*, Blue Star Art Space, San Antonio,
      TX (brochure)

SELECTED BIBILOGRAPHY

Atwell, Wendy Weil. "Chris Sauter: Pioneer," *ART LIES*, no. 52 (Fall 2006).
Baker, R.C. "Best in Show, Zeitgeist," *Village Voice*, 15 March 2007.
Colpitt, Frances. "Chris Sauter at ArtPace," *Art in America* 88 (February 2000).
Conolly, Maeve. "Limerick: EV+A," *Circa*, no. 112 (Summer 2005).
Cotter, Holland. "Where Drawing is What Counts," *New York Times*, 25 June 2005.
Ewing, John "Chris Sauter: Just Married," *ART LIES*, no. 45 (Winter 2005).
Gupta, Anjali. "Chris Sauter," *Art Papers* 30 (November / December 2006).
LaBelle, Charles. "Generation Z," *Frieze*, no. 48 (September / October 1999).
Perree, Rob. "Chris Sauter," *Kunstbeeld* 10 (September 2005).
Princenthal, Nancy. "Generation Z: Slacker Than Thou," *Art in America* 87
      (October 1999).

Chris Sauter
Tower II, detail, 2008
Wheat and glue
36 x 10 x 36"

POLLY LANNING SPARROW

Until recently, Polly Lanning Sparrow (born 1961) was best known as an abstract painter. Rather than canvas, she preferred birch plywood, a silky, cream-colored wood, squares of which she stacked and glued to create thick veneered supports. She subsequently turned the paintings' surfaces to the wall where their colors were reflected and now utilizes the floor as well as the wall, sliding rectangles of color into "real space." Crisp, luminous bands of color are encased or trapped between and behind the boards in a highly structural manner, recalling "actual bits of displaced architecture," according to Ann Reynolds. Lanning Sparrow received her BFA and MFA from UT-Austin and has been an artist-in-residence at Ucross, Chinati, and the Vermont Studio School. She lives and works in Austin.

EDUCATION

1995 MFA, University of Texas at Austin, Austin, TX
1992 BFA, University of Texas at Austin, Austin, TX
1983 BA, University of Texas at Austin, Austin, TX

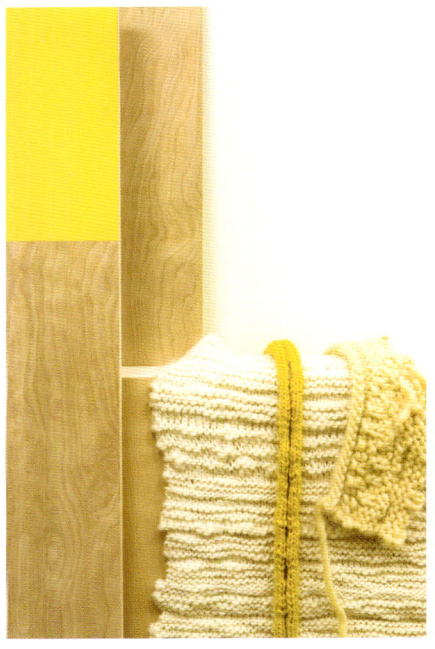

SELECTED INDIVIDUAL EXHIBITIONS

2004 *Solo Exhibition*, Gallery Materia, Scottsdale, AZ
2001 *Recent Work*, Rudolph Projects, Houston, TX
2000 *Parallels*, Women and Their Work, Austin, TX (catalogue)
    Locker Plant Paintings from Marfa, Rudolph Poissant Gallery, Houston, TX
1994 *New Paintings*, The New Gallery, University of Texas at Austin, Austin, TX

SELECTED GROUP EXHIBITIONS

2007 *Few, Some, Several, Many, and More*, Creative Research Lab, University of Texas at Austin, Austin, TX
2006 *New American Talent*, Arthouse at the Jones Center, Austin, TX (catalogue)
2004 *Winter Show*, d Berman Gallery, Austin, TX
    100 Drawings, Haggerty Gallery, University of Dallas, Irving, TX
2002 *Snap*, Dunn and Brown Contemporary, Dallas, TX
    Stall, Haggerty Gallery, The University of Dallas, Irving, TX
2001 *Mas! Mas! Mas!*, Gallery Lombardi, Austin, TX (catalogue)
1998 *It's About Design*, Women and Their Work, Austin, TX
1996 *Abstract Ideas of Painting*, Slover McCutcheon Gallery, Houston, TX
1994 *Contemporary Painting*, Cheekwood Museum of Art, Nashville, TN (catalogue)
1993 *Drawing into the 90s*, Laguna Gloria Art Museum, Austin, TX (catalogue)

SELECTED BIBLIOGRAPHY

Bae, James. "A Review of Arthouse's New American Talent 21," *...might be good*, no. 72, 30 June 2006 (http://www.fluentcollab.org).
Douberly, Amanda. "The 21st New American Talent Exhibit," *Austin Chronicle*, 14 July 2006.
Everett, Deborah. "Austin Artists Revisited," *NY Arts Magazine*, July 2002.
Keres, Alana. "Terra Lucida," *Tribeza*, November 2002.
Kutner, Janet. "Quick Draw: Impulsive Show Shines Light on Rising Stars," *Dallas Morning News*, 30 March 2002.
Petley, Kate. "Polly Lanning," *ART LIES*, no. 18 (Spring 1998).
Van Ryzin, Jeanne Claire. "Lanning's [...] Paintings [...], "*Austin American-Statesman*, 20 March 1999.

Polly Lanning Sparrow
Poulan (Redux), detail, 2008
Latex paint on birch plywood with wool
54 x 24 x 24"

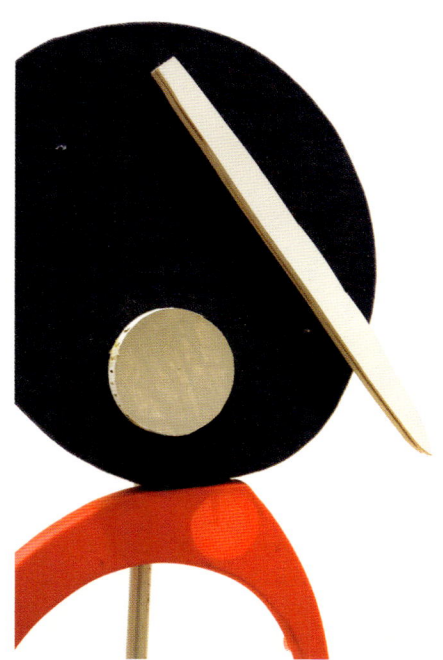

BRAD TUCKER

With a low-tech approach to cast-off, unlovely materials, Brad Tucker (born 1965) creates surprisingly beautiful objects. Inspired by pop music, many of his early works represent record players, speakers, and guitar amplifiers, fashioned from colorful fabric and scraps of wood. Utilizing similar materials, he has recently veered toward enigmatic abstractions, scaled to the human body—including its reach and grasp—but otherwise without literal meaning. Reviving his interest in music and musical instruments, the artist has expanded his aesthetic ambitions to include performance art, a well received example of which was presented at the opening reception for *Material Culture*. Tucker, who was born in Southern California and currently lives in Austin, has a BFA in painting and drawing from UNT and was a Core Fellow at the Glassell School of Art, Museum of Fine Arts, Houston, from 1999 – 2001.

EDUCATION

1991 BFA, University of North Texas, Denton, TX

SELECTED INDIVIDUAL EXHIBITIONS

2008 Art Palace, Austin, TX
      Inman Gallery, Houston, TX
2005 *Night and Day*, Inman Gallery, Houston, TX
2004 Mark Moore Gallery, Santa Monica, CA
      Arthouse at the Jones Center, Austin, TX
2003 *Present Future*, ARTissima 10, Turin, Italy
      Long Distance Lovers, Inman Gallery, Houston, TX
2002 *Boom*, Chicago, IL
      Singles, The Suburban, Chicago, IL
      Flip Flop, Lombard-Freid Fine Art, New York, NY
      The Verge: Brad Tucker, Plains Art Museum, Fargo, ND
      Ray Gun
2001 *Drum Solos*, Inman Gallery, Houston, TX
2000 *Brad Tucker*, Angstrom Gallery, Dallas, TX

SELECTED GROUP EXHIBITIONS

2007 *Texas Biennial*, Space 1808, City of Austin, Austin, TX
2006 *Fresh*, Elizabeth Leach Gallery, Portland, OR
2005 *Bill Davenport, Francesca Fuchs, Brad Tucker*, Ibid Projects, London, England
      Color/Pattern/Grid: Selections from the Austin Museum of Art and Austin Collections, Austin Museum of Art, Austin, TX
2004 *Rock*, Mark Moore Gallery, Santa Monica, CA
      Twang: Contemporary Sculpture From Texas, Art Museum of Southeast Texas, Beaumont, TX; McKinney Avenue Contemporary, Dallas, TX (catalogue)
      Treble, SculptureCenter, New York, NY
2003 *I Heart Texas*, Allston Skirt Gallery, Boston, MA
      Brad Tucker & Todd Hebert, Sala Diaz, San Antonio, TX
      Come Forward: Emerging Artists from Texas, Dallas Museum of Art, Dallas, TX (catalogue)
      Beyond the Academy: Encouraging New Talent From Texas, Arthouse at the Jones Center, Austin, TX (catalogue)
2002 *Hard Core*, Galveston Arts Center, Galveston, TX
      LISTE '02, Lombard-Fried Fine Arts, Basel, Switzerland
      Blip, Contemporary Art Museum of the University of South Florida, Tampa, FL
2001 *Off The Wall*, Gallery 400, University of Illinois at Chicago, Chicago, IL
      2001 Core Artists in Residence Exhibition, Glassell School of Art, Museum of Fine Arts, Houston, TX (catalogue)
      Armory Show, New York, NY
      Art Chicago 2001, Inman Gallery, Chicago, IL
2000 *Some New Minds*, P.S. 1 Contemporary Art Center, Long Island City, NY
      Stempo (two-person exhibition with Stephen Fritsch), Homeroom, Munich, Germany
      HiJinx, Arlington Museum of Art, Arlington, TX; University of Texas at Dallas, Dallas, TX
      2000 Core Artists in Residence Exhibition, Glassell School of Art, Museum of Fine Arts, Houston, TX (catalogue)
1998 *Jeff Elrod, Mark Flood, Brad Tucker*, Angstrom Gallery, Dallas, TX
1993 *STUFF*, 2X4 Art Gallery, Austin, TX
1990 *No Dogs*, UNT Union Art Gallery, University of North Texas, Denton, TX

SELECTED BIBLIOGRAPHY

Anspon, Catherine. "10 Year Anniversary Exhibition," *ART LIES*, no. 28 (Fall 2000).
Colpitt, Frances. "Space City Takes Off," *Art in America* 88 (October 2000).
Cox, Christopher, "'Treble': SculptureCenter, New York," *Artforum* 43 (September 2004).
Davenport, Bill. "Brad Tucker at Inman Gallery, Tire Iron #15," *Glasstire: Texas Visual Arts Online*, June 2001 (http://live.glasstire.com).
Ewing, John. "Treble: SculptureCenter," *ART LIES*, no. 43 (Summer 2004).
Hebert, Todd. "Brad Tucker at Angstrom Gallery," *ART LIES*, no. 33 (Winter 2000 – 2001).
Klaasmeyer, Kelly. "Idiot Savant," *Houston Press*, 5 – 11 June 2003.
Jankauskas, Jennifer. "Come Forward: Emerging Art in Texas " *ART LIES*, no.38 (Spring 2003).
Johnson, Patricia C. "Downtown Shows Feature Seascapes and Urban Life," *Houston Chronicle*, 24 May 2003.
_____. "Going Back To School," *Houston Chronicle*, 15 August 1999.
Johnson, Ken. "Brad Tucker, 'Flip Flop,'" *New York Times*, 18 January 2002.
Klaasmeyer, Kelly. "De-Meaning Objects," *Houston Press*, 29 June – 5 July 2000.
Kutner, Janet. "DMA Hooks Up With Young Artists," *Dallas Morning News*, 9 March 2003.
_____. "'Hi Jinx' Targets Art Forms, Life Forms," *Dallas Morning News*, 9 April 2000.
Newhall, Edith. "Dude, Where's My Art?" *New York Magazine*, 21–28 January 2002.

Brad Tucker
Open Globe, detail, 2007
Fabric, acrylic on wood and aluminum
13 x 39 x 9"